AF540924

The Principles of Rabindranath Tagore

The Principles of Rabindranath Tagore

Parameshwar Hegde
M.Sc., M.A.

Neha Publishers & Distributors
4832/24, Prahlad Lane, S-207 Ansari Raod, Daryaganj, New Delhi-110002

Published by
Neha Publishers & Distributors
4832/24, Prahlad Lane, S-207 Ansari Raod, Daryaganj,
New Delhi-110002
Tel.: 011-43570976, 23278261,
Email-nehapubdistributors@gmail.com

First Edition : 2013

ISBN : 978-93-80318-21-9

Price : 325/-

Laser Typesetting by : Tamalika Computers, Delhi

Printed at: Nagri Printers, Delhi

PRINTED IN INDIA

Published by Neha Publishers & Distributors, New Delhi-110002

Preface

Rabindranath Tagore , sobriquet Gurudev, was an Indian Bengali polymath. He was a popular poet, novelist, musician, and playwright who reshaped Bengali literature and music in the late 19th and early 20th centuries. As author of *Gitanjali* and its "profoundly sensitive, fresh and beautiful verse", and as the first Asian to win the Nobel Prize in Literature, Tagore was perhaps the most widely regarded Indian literary figure of all time. He was a mesmerizing representative of the Indian culture whose influence and popularity internationally perhaps could only be compared to that of Gandhi, whom Tagore named 'Mahatma' out of his deep admiration for him.

A Pirali Brahmin from Kolkata, Tagore was already writing poems at age eight. At age sixteen, he published his first substantial poetry under the pseudonym *Bhanushingho* ("Sun Lion") and wrote his first short stories and dramas in 1877. Tagore denounced the British Raj and supported independence. His efforts endure in his vast canon and in the institution he founded, Visva-Bharati University.

Tagore modernised Bengali art by spurning rigid classical forms. His novels, stories, songs, dance-dramas, and essays spoke to political and personal topics. *Gitanjali* (*Song Offerings*), *Gora* (*Fair-Faced*), and *Ghare-Baire* (*The Home and the World*) are his best-known works, and his verse, short stories, and novels were acclaimed for their lyricism, colloquialism, naturalism, and contemplation. Tagore was perhaps the only litterateur who penned anthems of two countries: India and Bangladesh: *Jana Gana Mana* and *Amar Shonar Bangla*.

Tagore's last four years were marked by chronic pain and two long periods of illness. These began when Tagore lost consciousness in late 1937; he remained comatose and near death for an extended period. This was followed three years later, in late 1940, by a similar spell, from which he never recovered. The poetry Tagore wrote in these years is among his finest, and is distinctive for its preoccupation with death. After extended suffering, Tagore died on 7 August 1941 (22 Shravan 1348) in an upstairs room of the Jorasanko mansion in which he was raised; his death anniversary is mourned across the Bengali-speaking world.

Via translations, Tagore influenced Hispanic literature: Chileans Pablo Neruda and Gabriela Mistral, Mexican writer Octavio Paz, and Spaniards José Ortega y Gasset, Zenobia Camprubí, and Juan Ramón Jiménez. Between 1914 and 1922, the Jiménez-Camprubí spouses translated twenty-two of Tagore's books from English into Spanish and extensively revised and adapted such works as Tagore's *The Crescent Moon*. In this time, Jiménez developed "naked poetry" (Spanish: «poesia desnuda»), a landmark innovation. Ortega y Gasset wrote that "Tagore's wide appeal [may stem from the fact that] he speaks of longings for perfection that we all have ... Tagore awakens a dormant sense of childish wonder, and he saturates the air with all kinds of enchanting promises for the reader, who ... pays little attention to the deeper import of Oriental mysticism". Tagore's works circulated in free editions around 1920 alongside those of Dante Alighieri, Miguel de Cervantes, Johann Wolfgang von Goethe, Plato, and Leo Tolstoy.

Tagore was deemed overrated by some Westerners. Graham Greene doubted that "anyone but Mr. Yeats can still take his poems very seriously." Modern remnants of a past Latin American reverence of Tagore were discovered, for example, by an astonished Salman Rushdie during a trip to Nicaragua.

Parameshwar Hegde
M.Sc.,M.A.

Contents

1

INTRODUCTION

Rabindranath Tagore (7 May 1861 – 7 August 1941), so briquet Gurudev, was an Indian Bengali polymath. He was a popular poet, novelist, musician, and playwright who reshaped Bengali literature and music in the late 19th and early 20th centuries. As author of *Gitanjali* and its "profoundly sensitive, fresh and beautiful verse", and as the first Asian to win the Nobel Prize in Literature, Tagore was perhaps the most widely regarded Indian literary figure of all time. He was a mesmerizing representative of the Indian culture whose influence and popularity internationally perhaps could only be compared to that of Gandhi, whom Tagore named 'Mahatma' out of his deep admiration for him.

A Pirali Brahmin from Kolkata, Tagore was already writing poems at age eight. At age sixteen, he published his first substantial poetry under the pseudonym *Bhanushingho* ("Sun Lion") and wrote his first short stories and dramas in 1877. Tagore denounced the British Raj and supported independence. His efforts endure in his vast canon and in the institution he founded, Visva-Bharati University.

Tagore modernised Bengali art by spurning rigid classical forms. His novels, stories, songs, dance-dramas, and essays spoke to political and personal topics. *Gitanjali* (*Song Offerings*), *Gora* (*Fair-Faced*), and *Ghare-Baire* (*The Home and the World*) are his best-known works, and his verse, short stories, and novels were acclaimed for their lyricism, colloquialism, naturalism, and contemplation. Tagore was perhaps the only litterateur who penned anthems of two countries: India and Bangladesh: *Jana Gana Mana* and *Amar Shonar Bangla*.

The youngest of thirteen surviving children, Tagore was born in the Jorasanko mansion in Kolkata of parents Debendranath Tagore (1817–1905) and Sarada Devi (1830–1875). Tagore family patriarchs were the Brahmo founding fathers of the Adi Dharm faith. He was mostly raised by servants, as his mother had died in his early childhood; his father travelled extensively. Tagore largely declined classroom schooling, preferring to roam the mansion or nearby idylls: Bolpur, Panihati, and others. Upon his *upanayan* initiation at age eleven, Tagore left Kolkata on 14 February 1873 to tour India with his father for several months. They visited his father's Santiniketan estate and stopped in Amritsar before reaching the Himalayan hill station of Dalhousie. There, young "Rabi" read biographies and was home-educated in history, astronomy, modern science, and Sanskrit, and examined the poetry of Kalidasa. He completed major works in 1877, one a long poem of the Maithili style pioneered by Vidyapati. Published pseudonymously, experts accepted them as the lost works of Bhanusi?ha, a newly discovered 17th-century Vai??ava poet. He wrote "Bhikharini" (1877; "The Beggar Woman"—the Bengali language's first short story) and *Sandhya Sangit* (1882)—including the famous poem "Nirjharer Swapnabhanga" ("The Rousing of the Waterfall").

A prospective barrister, Tagore enrolled at a public school in Brighton, East Sussex, England in 1878. He read law at University College London, but left school to explore Shakespeare and more: *Religio Medici*, *Coriolanus*, and *Antony and Cleopatra*; he returned degreeless to Bengal in 1880. On 9 December 1883 he married Mrinalini Devi (born Bhabatarini, 1873–1900); they had five children, two of whom died before reaching adulthood. In 1890, Tagore began managing his family's vast estates in Shilaidaha, a region now in Bangladesh; he was joined by his wife and children in 1898. In 1890, Tagore released his *Manasi* poems, among his best-known work. As "Zamindar Babu",

Tagore crisscrossed the holdings while living out of the family's luxurious barge, the *Padma*, to collect (mostly token) rents and bless villagers, who held feasts in his honour. These years—1891–1895: Tagore's *Sadhana* period, after one of Tagore's magazines—were his most fecund. During this period, more than half the stories of the three-volume and eighty-four-story *Galpaguchchha* were written. With irony and gravity, they depicted a wide range of Bengali lifestyles, particularly village life.

Fig 1.1 *Rabindranath Tagore*

In 1901, Tagore left Shilaidaha and moved to Shantiniketan to found an *ashram* which grew to include a marble-floored prayer hall ("The *Mandir*"), an experimental school, groves of trees, gardens, and a library. There, Tagore's wife and two of his children died. His father died on 19 January 1905. He received monthly payments as part of his inheritance and additional income from the Maharaja of Tripura, sales of his family's jewellery, his seaside bungalow in Puri, and mediocre royaltics (Rs. 2,000) from his works. By now, his work was gaining him a large following among Bengali and foreign readers alike, and he published such works as *Naivedya* (1901) and *Kheya*

(1906) while translating his poems into free verse. On 14 November 1913, Tagore learned that he had won the 1913 Nobel Prize in Literature, becoming the first Asian Nobel laureate. The Swedish Academy appreciated the idealistic and—for Western readers—accessible nature of a small body of his translated material, including the 1912 *Gitanjali: Song Offerings*. In 1915, Tagore was knighted by the British Crown. He later returned his knighthood in protest of the massacre of unarmed Indians in 1919 at Jallianwala Bagh.

In 1921, Tagore and agricultural economist Leonard Elmhirst set up the Institute for Rural Reconstruction, later renamed Shriniketan—"Abode of Peace"—in Surul, a village near the ashram at Santiniketan. Through it, Tagore bypassed Gandhi's symbolic *Swaraj* protests, which he despised. He sought aid from donors, officials, and scholars worldwide to "free village[s] from the shackles of helplessness and ignorance" by "vitalis[ing] knowledge". In the early 1930s, he targeted India's "abnormal caste consciousness" and untouchability. Lecturing against these, he penned untouchable heroes for his poems and dramas and campaigned—successfully—to open Guruvayoor Temple to Dalits.

To the end, Tagore scrutinized orthodoxy. He upbraided Gandhi for declaring that a massive 15 January 1934 earthquake in Bihar—leaving thousands dead—was divine retribution brought on by the oppression of Dalits. He mourned the endemic poverty of Kolkata and the accelerating socioeconomic decline of Bengal, which he detailed in an unrhymed hundred-line poem whose technique of searing double-vision would foreshadow Satyajit Ray's film *Apur Sansar*. Fifteen new volumes of Tagore writings appeared, among them the prose-poems works *Punashcha* (1932), *Shes Saptak* (1935), and *Patraput* (1936). Experimentation continued: he developed prose-songs and dance-dramas, including *Chitrangada* (1914), *Shyama* (1939), and *Chandalika* (1938), and wrote the novels *Dui Bon* (1933), *Malancha* (1934), and *Char Adhyay* (1934). Tagore took an interest in science in his last years, writing *Visva-Parichay* (a collection of essays) in 1937. His exploration of biology, physics, and astronomy impacted his poetry, which often contained extensive naturalism that underscored his respect for scientific laws. He also wove the process of science, including narratives of scientists, into many stories contained in such volumes as *Se* (1937), *Tin Sangi* (1940), and *Galpasalpa* (1941).

Tagore's last four years were marked by chronic pain and two long periods of illness. These began when Tagore lost consciousness in late 1937; he remained comatose and near death for an extended period. This was followed three years later, in late 1940, by a similar spell, from which he never recovered. The poetry Tagore wrote in these years is among his finest, and is distinctive for its preoccupation with death. After extended suffering, Tagore died on 7 August 1941 (22 Shravan 1348) in an upstairs room of the Jorasanko mansion in which he was raised; his death anniversary is mourned across the Bengali-speaking world.

Between 1878 and 1932, Tagore visited more than thirty countries on five continents; many of these trips were crucial in familiarising non-Indian audiences with his works and spreading his political ideas. In 1912, he took a sheaf of his translated works to England, where they impressed missionary and Gandhi protégé Charles F. Andrews,Irish poet William Butler Yeats, Ezra Pound, Robert Bridges, Ernest Rhys, Thomas Sturge Moore, and others. Indeed, Yeats wrote the preface to the English translation of *Gitanjali*, while Andrews joined Tagore at Santiniketan. On 10 November 1912, Tagore began touring the United States and the United Kingdom, staying in Butterton, Staffordshire with Andrews's clergymen friends. From 3 May 1916 until April 1917, Tagore went on lecturing circuits in Japan and the United States and denounced nationalism. His essay "Nationalism in India" was scorned and praised, this latter by pacifists, including Romain Rolland.

Fig 1.2 *Tagore and Mrinalini Devi, 1883*

Shortly after returning to India, the 63-year-old Tagore accepted the Peruvian government's invitation to visit. He then travelled to Mexico. Each government pledged US$100,000 to the school at Shantiniketan (Visva-Bharati) in commemoration of his visits. A week after his 6 November 1924 arrival in Buenos Aires, Argentina, an ill Tagore moved into the Villa Miralrío at the behest of Victoria Ocampo. He left for India in January 1925. On 30 May 1926, Tagore reached Naples, Italy; he met Benito Mussolini in Rome the next day. A warm rapport ended when Tagore criticised Mussolini on 20 July 1926.

On 14 July 1927, Tagore and two companions began a four-month tour of Southeast Asia, visiting Bali, Java, Kuala Lumpur, Malacca, Penang, Siam, and Singapore. Tagore's travelogues from the tour were collected into the work "Jatri". In early 1930 he left Bengal for a nearly year-long tour of Europe and the United States. Once he returned to the UK, while his paintings were being exhibited in Paris and London, he stayed at a Friends settlement in Birmingham. There he wrote his Oxford Hibbert Lectures and spoke at London's annual Quaker gathering. There (addressing relations between the British and Indians, a topic he would grapple with over the next two years), Tagore spoke of a "dark chasm of aloofness". He visited Aga Khan III, stayed at Dartington Hall, and toured Denmark, Switzerland, and Germany from June to mid-September 1930, then the Soviet Union. Lastly, in April 1932, Tagore—who was acquainted with the legends and works of the Persian mystic Hafez—was hosted by Reza Shah Pahlavi of Iran. Such extensive travels allowed Tagore to interact with many notable contemporaries, including Henri Bergson, Albert Einstein, Robert Frost, Thomas Mann, George Bernard Shaw, H.G. Wells and Romain Rolland. Tagore's last travels abroad, including visits to Persia and Iraq (in 1932) and Ceylon (in 1933), only sharpened his opinions regarding human divisions and nationalism.

Fig 1.3 *Tagore in Berlin, 1930*

Though known mostly for his poetry, Tagore also wrote novels, essays, short stories, travelogues, dramas, and thousands of songs. Of Tagore's prose, his short stories are perhaps most highly regarded; indeed, he is credited with originating the Bengali-language version of the genre. His works are frequently noted for their rhythmic, optimistic, and lyrical nature.

Such stories mostly borrow from deceptively simple subject matter: common people.

Tagore wrote eight novels and four novellas, among them *Chaturanga, Shesher Kobita, Char Odhay,* and *Noukadubi. Ghare Baire* (*The Home and the World*)—through the lens of the idealistic *zamindar* protagonist Nikhil—excoriates rising Indian nationalism, terrorism, and religious zeal in the *Swadeshi* movement; a frank expression of Tagore's conflicted sentiments, it emerged out of a 1914 bout of depression. The novel ends in Hindu-Muslim violence and Nikhil's (likely mortal) wounding. *Gora* raises controversial questions regarding the Indian identity. As with *Ghare Baire,* matters of self-identity (*jati*) personal freedom, and religion are developed in the context of a family story and love triangle.

In *Jogajog* (*Relationships*), the heroine Kumudini—bound by the ideals of *Siva-Sati,* exemplified by Dakshayani—is torn between her pity for the sinking fortunes of her progressive and compassionate elder brother and his foil: her exploitative, rakish, and patriarchical husband. In it, Tagore demonstrates his feminist leanings, using *pathos* to depict the plight and ultimate demise of Bengali women trapped by pregnancy, duty, and family honour; simultaneously, he treats the decline of Bengal's landed oligarchy.

Others were uplifting: *Shesher Kobita* (translated twice as *Last Poem* and *Farewell Song*) is his most lyrical novel, with poems and rhythmic passages written by the main character, a poet. It also contains elements of satire and postmodernism; stock characters gleefully attack the reputation of an old, outmoded, oppressively renowned poet who, incidentally, goes by the name of Rabindranath Tagore. Though his novels remain among the least-appreciated of his works, they have been given renewed attention via film adaptations by Satyajit Ray and others: *Chokher Bali* and *Ghare Baire* are exemplary. Their soundtracks often feature *rabindras git*.

Tagore wrote many non-fiction books, writing on topics ranging from Indian history to linguistics to spirituality. Aside from autobiographical works, his travelogues, essays, and lectures were compiled into several volumes, including *Europe Jatrir Patro* (*Letters from Europe*) and *Manusher Dhormo*

Fig 1.4 *Tagore with Einstein, 1930*

Tagore composed roughly 2,230 songs and was a prolific painter. His songs comprise *rabindrasangit* "Tagore Song"), an integral part of Bengali culture. Tagore's music is inseparable from his literature, most of which—poems or parts of novels, stories, or plays alike—became lyrics for his songs. Influenced by the *thumri* style of Hindustani music, they ran the entire gamut of human emotion, ranging from his early dirge-like Brahmo devotional hymns to quasi-erotic compositions. They emulated the tonal color of classical *ragas* to varying extents. Though at times his songs mimicked a given raga's melody and rhythm faithfully, he also blended elements of different ragas to create innovative works.

For Bengalis, their appeal, stemming from the combination of emotive strength and beauty described as surpassing even Tagore's poetry, was such that the *Modern Review* observed that "[t]here is in Bengal no cultured home where Rabindranath's songs are not sung or at least attempted to be sung ... Even illiterate villagers sing his songs". Arthur Strangways of *The*

Observer introduced non-Bengalis to *rabindrasangeet* in *The Music of Hindostan*, calling it a "vehicle of a personality ... [that] go behind this or that system of music to that beauty of sound which all systems put out their hands to seize." Among them are Bangladesh's national anthem *Amar Shonar Bangla* which became the national anthem of Bangladesh in the year 1971 and India's national anthem *Jana Gana Mana* is written in the year 1911 , making Tagore unique in having scored two national anthems. He influenced the styles of such musicians as *sitar* maestro Vilayat Khan, and the *sarodiyas* Buddhadev Dasgupta and Amjad Ali Khan.

At age sixty, Tagore took up drawing and painting; successful exhibitions of his many works—which made a debut appearance in Paris upon encouragement by artists he met in the south of France —were held throughout Europe. Tagore—who likely exhibited protanopia ("color blindness"), or partial

Fig 1.5 *Tagore dabbled in primitivism: a pastel-coloured rendition of a Malagan mask from northern New Ireland*

lack of (red-green, in Tagore's case) colour discernment—painted in a style characterised by peculiarities in aesthetics and colouring schemes. Tagore emulated numerous styles, including craftwork from northern New Ireland, Haida carvings from the west coast of Canada (British Columbia), and woodcuts by Max Pechstein. Tagore also had an artist's eye for his own handwriting, embellishing the scribbles, cross-outs, and word layouts in his manuscripts with simple artistic leitmotifs, including simple rhythmic designs.

At age sixteen, Tagore led his brother Jyotirindranath's adaptation of Molière's *Le Bourgeois Gentilhomme*. At age twenty, he wrote his first drama-opera—*Valmiki Pratibha* (*The Genius of Valmiki*)—which describes how the bandit Valmiki reforms his ethos, is blessed by Saraswati, and composes the *Ramayana*. Through it, Tagore vigorously explores a wide range of dramatic styles and emotions, including usage of revamped *kirtans* and adaptation of traditional English and Irish folk melodies as drinking songs. Another notable play, *Dak Ghar* (*The Post Office*), describes how a child—striving to escape his stuffy confines—ultimately "fall[s] asleep" (which suggests his physical death). A story with worldwide appeal (it received rave reviews in Europe), *Dak Ghar* dealt with death as, in Tagore's words, "spiritual freedom" from "the world of hoarded wealth and certified creeds". During World War II, Polish doctor and educator Janusz Korczak selected "The Post Office" as the play the orphans in his care in the Warsaw Ghetto would perform. This occurred on 18 July 1942, less than three weeks before they were to be deported to the Treblinka extermination camp. According to his main English-language biographer, Betty Jean Lifton, in her book *The King of Children*, Dr. Korszak thought a great deal about whether one should be able to determine when and how to die. He may have been trying to find a way for the children in his orphanage to accept death.

His other works—emphasizing fusion of lyrical flow and emotional rhythm tightly focused on a core idea—were unlike previous Bengali dramas. His works sought to articulate, in

Tagore's words, "the play of feeling and not of action". In 1890 he wrote *Visarjan* (*Sacrifice*), regarded as his finest drama. The Bengali-language originals included intricate subplots and extended monologues. Later, his dramas probed more philosophical and allegorical themes; these included *Dak Ghar*. Another is Tagore's *Chandalika* (*Untouchable Girl*), which was modeled on an ancient Buddhist legend describing how Ananda—the Gautama Buddha's disciple—asks water of an *Adivasi* (belonging to an indigenous tribe) girl. Lastly, among his most famous dramas is *Raktakaravi* (*Red Oleanders*), which tells of a kleptocratic king who enriches himself by forcing his subjects to mine. The heroine, Nandini, eventually rallies the common people to destroy these symbols of subjugation. Tagore's other plays include *Chitrangada, Raja,* and *Mayar Khela*. Dance dramas based on Tagore's plays are commonly referred to as *rabindra nritya natyas*.

Fig 1.6 *A Nandalal Bose illustration for "The Hero", part of the 1913 Macmillan release of The Crescent Moon.*

The "Sadhana" period, 1891–1895, was among Tagore's most fecund, yielding more than half the stories contained in the three-volume *Galpaguchchha*, itself a group of eighty-four stories. They reflect upon Tagore's surroundings, on modern and fashionable ideas, and on mind puzzles. Tagore associated his earliest stories, such as those of the "*Sadhana*" period, with an exuberance of vitality and spontaneity; these traits were cultivated by zamindar Tagore's life in villages such as Patisar, Shajadpur, and Shilaida. Seeing the common and the poor, he examined their lives with a depth and feeling singular in Indian literature up to that point.

In "The Fruitseller from Kabul", Tagore speaks in first person as a town-dweller and novelist who chances upon the Afghani seller. He channels the longing of those trapped in mundane, hardscrabble Indian urban life, giving play to dreams of a different existence in the distant and wild mountains: "There were autumn mornings, the time of year when kings of old went forth to conquest; and I, never stirring from my little corner in Kolkata, would let my mind wander over the whole world. At the very name of another country, my heart would go out to it ... I would fall to weaving a network of dreams: the mountains, the glens, the forest .... ". Many of the other *Galpaguchchha* stories were written in Tagore's *Sabuj Patra* period (1914–1917; also named for one of Tagore's magazines).

Tagore's *Golpoguchchho* (*Bunch of Stories*) remains among Bengali literature's most popular fictional works, providing subject matter for many successful films and theatrical plays. Satyajit Ray's film *Charulata* was based upon Tagore's controversial novella, *Nastanirh* (*The Broken Nest*). In *Atithi* (also made into a film), the young Brahmin boy Tarapada shares a boat ride with a village *zamindar*. The boy reveals that he has run away from home, only to wander around ever since. Taking pity, the zamindar adopts him and ultimately arranges his marriage to the *zamindar's* own daughter. However, the night before the wedding, Tarapada runs off—again. *Strir Patra* (*The Letter from the Wife*) is among Bengali literature's earliest depictions of the bold emancipation of women. The heroine Mrinal, the wife of a typical patriarchical Bengali middle class man, writes a letter while she is travelling (which constitutes the whole story). It details the pettiness of her life and struggles; she finally declares that she will not return to her husband's home with the statement *Amio bachbo. Ei bachlum*: "And I shall live. Here, I live".

Haimanti assails Hindu marriage and the dismal lifelessness of married Bengali women, hypocrisies plaguing the Indian middle classes, and how Haimanti, a sensitive young woman, must—due to her sensitiveness and free spirit—sacrifice her life. In the last passage, Tagore directly attacks the Hindu custom of glorifying Sita's attempted self-immolation as a means of appeasing her husband Rama's doubts. *Musalmani Didi* examines Hindu-Muslim tensions and, in many ways, embodies the essence of Tagore's humanism. *Darpaharan* exhibits Tagore's self-consciousness, describing a fey young man harboring literary ambitions. Though he loves his wife, he wishes to stifle her own literary career, deeming it unfeminine. Tagore himself, in his youth, seems to have harbored similar ideas about women. *Darpaharan* depicts the final humbling of the man as he acknowledges his wife's talents. As do many other Tagore stories, *Jibito o Mrito* equips Bengalis with a ubiquitous epigram: *Kadombini moriya proman korilo she more nai*—"Kadombini died, thereby proving that she hadn't".

Tagore's poetry—which varied in style from classical formalism to the comic, visionary, and ecstatic—proceeds from a lineage established by 15th- and 16th-century Vaishnava poets. Tagore was awed by the mysticism of the *rishi*-authors who—including Vyasa—wrote the Upanishads, the Bhakti-Sufi mystic Kabir, and Ramprasad Sen. Yet Tagore's poetry became most innovative and mature after his exposure to rural Bengal's folk music, which included Baul ballads—especially those of bard Lalon. These—rediscovered and popularised by Tagore—resemble 19th-century Kartabhaja hymns that emphasize inward divinity and rebellion against religious and social orthodoxy. During his Shilaidaha years, his poems took on a lyrical quality, speaking via the *maner manus* (the Bauls' "man within the heart") or meditating upon the *jivan devata* ("living God within"). This figure thus sought connection with divinity through appeal to nature and the emotional interplay of human drama. Tagore used such techniques in his Bhanusi?ha poems (which chronicle the romance between Radha and Krishna), which he repeatedly revised over the course of seventy years.

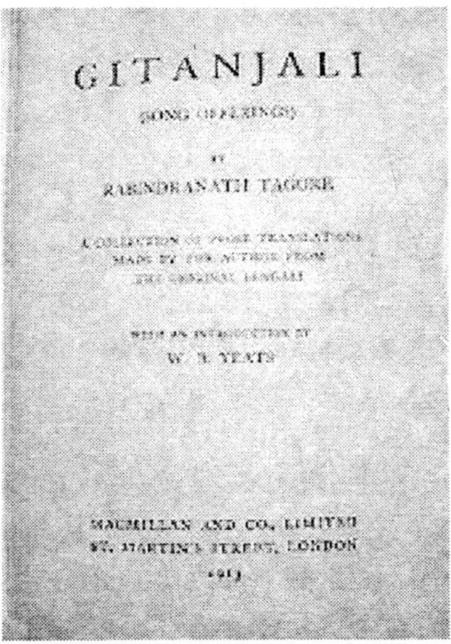

GITANJALI

RABINDRANATH TAGORE

W. B. YEATS

MACMILLAN AND CO., LIMITED
ST. MARTIN'S STREET, LONDON

Fig 1.7 *Title page of Gitanjali*

Tagore's poetry has been set to music by various composers, among them classical composer Arthur Shepherd's triptych for soprano and string quartet, as well as composer Garry Schyman's "Praan", an adaptation of Tagore's poem "Stream of Life" from Gitanjali. The latter was composed and recorded with vocals by Palbasha Siddique to accompany Internet celebrity Matt Harding's 2008 viral video. In 1917 his words were translated adeptly and set to music by Richard Hageman (an Anglo- Dutch composer) to produce what is regarded as one of the finest art songs in the English language: Do not go my love.

Tagore's political thought was complex. He opposed imperialism and supported Indian nationalists. His views have their first poetic release in *Manast*, mostly composed in his twenties. Evidence produced during the Hindu-German Conspiracy trial and later accounts affirm his awareness of the Ghadarite conspiracy, and stated that he sought the support of Japanese Prime Minister Terauchi Masatake and former Premier Okuma Shigenobu. Yet he lampooned the Swadeshi movement, denouncing it in "The Cult of the Charka", an acrid 1925 essay. He emphasized self-help and intellectual uplift of the masses as an alternative, stating that British imperialism was a "political symptom of our social disease", urging Indians to accept that "there can be no question of blind revolution, but of steady and purposeful education".

Such views enraged many. He narrowly escaped assassination by Indian expatriates during his stay in a San Francisco hotel in late 1916. The plot failed only because the would-be assassins fell into argument. Yet Tagore wrote songs lionizing the Indian independence movement and renounced his knighthood in protest against the 1919 Jallianwala Bagh Massacre. Two of Tagore's more politically charged compositions, "Chitto Jetha Bhayshunyo" ("Where the Mind is Without Fear") and "Ekla Chalo Re" ("If They Answer Not to Thy Call, Walk Alone"), gained mass appeal, with the latter favoured by Gandhi. Despite his tumultuous relations with Gandhi, Tagore was key in resolving a Gandhi-Ambedkar dispute involving separate electorates for untouchables, ending Gandhi's fast "unto death".

Fig 1.8 *Tagore hosts Gandhi and wife Kasturba at Santiniketan in 1940.*

Tagore's relevance can be gauged by festivals honouring him: *Kabipranam*, Tagore's birth anniversary; the annual Tagore Festival held in Urbana, Illinois, in the United States; *Rabindra Path Parikrama* walking pilgrimages from Kolkata to Shantiniketan; ceremonial recitals of Tagore's poetry held on important anniversaries; and others. This legacy is most palpable in Bengali culture, ranging from language and arts to history and politics. Nobel laureate Amartya Sen saw Tagore as a "towering figure", being a "deeply relevant and many-sided contemporary thinker". Tagore's Bengali-language writings—the 1939 *Rabindra Rachanavali*—is also canonised as one of Bengal's greatest cultural treasures. Tagore himself was proclaimed "the greatest poet India has produced".

Tagore lampooned rote schooling: in "The Parrot's Training", a bird is caged and force-fed pages torn from books until it dies. These views led Tagore, while visiting Santa Barbara on 11 October 1917, to conceive of a new type of university, desiring to "make Santiniketan the connecting thread between India and the world [and] a world center for the study of humanity somewhere beyond the limits of nation and geography." The school, which he named Visva-Bharati had its foundation stone laid on 22 December 1918; it was later inaugurated on 22 December 1921. Here, Tagore implemented a *brahmacharya* pedagogical structure employing *gurus* to provide individualised guidance for pupils. Tagore worked hard to fundraise for and staff the school, even contributing all of his Nobel Prize monies. Tagore's duties as steward and mentor at Santiniketan kept him busy; he taught classes in mornings and wrote the students' textbooks in afternoons and evenings. Tagore also fundraised extensively for the school in Europe and the U.S. between 1919 and 1921 .

Tagore was famed throughout much of Europe, North America, and East Asia. He co-founded Dartington Hall School, a progressive coeducational institution; in Japan, he influenced such figures as Nobel laureate Yasunari Kawabata. Tagore's works were widely translated into English, Dutch, German,

Spanish, and other European languages by Czech indologist Vincenc Lesný, French Nobel laureate André Gide, Russian poet Anna Akhmatova, former Turkish Prime Minister Bülent Ecevit, and others. In the United States, Tagore's lecturing circuits, particularly those in 1916–1917, were widely attended and acclaimed. Yet, several controversies involving Tagore resulted in a decline in his popularity in Japan and North America after the late 1920s, concluding with his "near total eclipse" outside of Bengal.

Fig 1.9 *Bust in Prague*

Via translations, Tagore influenced Hispanic literature: Chileans Pablo Neruda and Gabriela Mistral, Mexican writer Octavio Paz, and Spaniards José Ortega y Gasset, Zenobia Camprubí, and Juan Ramón Jiménez. Between 1914 and 1922, the Jiménez-Camprubí spouses translated twenty-two of Tagore's books from English into Spanish and extensively revised and adapted such works as Tagore's *The Crescent Moon*. In this time, Jiménez developed "naked poetry" (Spanish: «poesia desnuda»), a landmark innovation. Ortega y Gasset wrote that "Tagore's wide appeal [may stem from the fact that] he speaks of longings for perfection that we all have ... Tagore awakens a dormant sense of childish wonder, and he saturates the air with all kinds of enchanting promises for the reader, who ... pays little attention to the deeper import of Oriental mysticism". Tagore's works circulated in free editions around 1920 alongside those of Dante Alighieri, Miguel de Cervantes, Johann Wolfgang von Goethe, Plato, and Leo Tolstoy.

Tagore was deemed overrated by some Westerners. Graham Greene doubted that "anyone but Mr. Yeats can still take his poems very seriously." Modern remnants of a past Latin American reverence of Tagore were discovered, for example, by an astonished Salman Rushdie during a trip to Nicaragua.

2

BENGALI PEOPLE

The Bengali people are an ethnic community native to the historic region of Bengal (now divided between Bangladesh and India) in South Asia. They speak Bengali, which is an Indo-Aryan language of the eastern Indian subcontinent, evolved from the Magadhi Prakrit and Sanskrit languages. In their native language, they are referred to as (pronounced *Bangali*). They are an Indo-Aryan people, though they are also descended from Mongolo-Dravidians, closely related to Austro-Asiatic, Dravidian, Assamese, East Indian, Sinhalese, Munda and Tibeto-Burman peoples. As such, Bengalis are a homogeneous but considerably diverse ethnic group with heterogeneous origins.

They are mostly concentrated in Bangladesh and the states of West Bengal and Tripura in India. There are also a number of Bengali communities scattered across North-East India, New Delhi, and the Indian states of Assam, Jharkhand, Bihar, Maharastra, Karnataka, Andhra Pradesh, Madhya Pradesh, Uttar Pradesh and Orissa. In addition, there are significant Bengali communities beyond South Asia; some of the most well established Bengali communities are in the United Kingdom and United States. Large numbers of Bengalis (mainly from Sylhet) have settled in Britain, mainly living in the East boroughs of London, numbering from around 300,000; in the USA there are about 150,000 living across the country, mainly in New York. There are also millions living across the Gulf States, majority of whom are living as foreign workers. There also many Bengalis in Malaysia, South Korea, Canada, Japan, Australia and many other countries.

Remnants of civilisation in the greater Bengal region date back 4,000 years, when the region was settled by Dravidian, Tibeto-Burman and Austro-Asiatic peoples. The exact origin of the word *Bangla* or Bengal is unknown, though it is believed to be derived from the Dravidian-speaking tribe *Bang* that settled in the area around the year 1000 BCE.

After the arrival of Indo-Aryans, the kingdoms of Anga, Vanga and Magadha were formed in and around Bengal and were first described in the *Atharvaveda* around 1000 BCE. From the 6th century BCE, Magadha expanded to include most of the Bihar and Bengal regions. It was one of the four main kingdoms of India at the time of Buddha and was one of the sixteen Mahajanapadas. Under the Maurya Empire founded by Chandragupta Maurya, Magadha extended over nearly all of South Asia, including parts of Persia and Afghanistan, reaching its greatest extent under the Buddhist emperor Ashoka the Great in the 3rd century BCE. One of the earliest foreign references to Bengal is the mention of a land ruled by the king Xandrammes named Gangaridai by the Greeks around 100 BCE. The word is speculated to have come from *Gangahrd* (Land with the Ganges in its heart) in reference to an area in Bengal. Later from the 3rd to the 6th centuries CE, the kingdom of Magadha served as the seat of the Gupta Empire.

One of the first recorded independent king of Bengal was Shashanka, reigning around the early 7th century. After a period of anarchy, Gopala came to power in 750 by democratic election. He founded the Bengali Buddhist Pala Empire which ruled the region for four hundred years, and expanded across much of Southern Asia, from Assam in the northeast, to Kabul in the west, to Andhra Pradesh in the south. Atisha was a renowned Bengali Buddhist teacher who was instrumental in revival of Buddhism in Tibet and also held the position of Abbot at the Vikramshila university. Tilopa was also from Bengal region.

The Pala dynasty was later followed by a shorter reign of the Hindu Sena Empire. Islam was introduced to Bengal in the twelfth century by Sufi missionaries. Subsequent Muslim conquests helped spread Islam throughout the region. Bakhtiar Khilji, an Afghan general of the Slave dynasty of Delhi Sultanate, defeated Lakshman Sen of the Sena dynasty and conquered large parts of Bengal. Consequently, the region was ruled by dynasties of sultans and feudal lords under the Delhi Sultanate for the next few hundred years. Islam was introduced to the Sylhet region by the Muslim saint Shah Jalal in the early 14th century. In the early 17th century, Mughal general Islam Khan conquered Bengal. However, administration by governors appointed by the court of the Mughal Empire gave way to semi-independence of the area under the Nawabs of Murshidabad, who nominally respected the sovereignty of the Mughals in Delhi. After the weakening of the Mughal Empire with the death of Emperor Aurangzeb in 1707, Bengal was ruled independently by the Nawabs until 1757, when the region was annexed by the East India Company after the Battle of Plassey.

The Bengal Renaissance refers to a social reform movement during the nineteenth and early twentieth centuries in the region of Bengal in undivided India during the period of British rule. The Bengal renaissance can be said to have started with Raja Ram Mohan Roy (1775-1833) and ended with Rabindranath Tagore (1861-1941), although there have been many stalwarts thereafter embodying particular aspects of the unique intellectual and creative output. Nineteenth century Bengal was a unique blend of religious and social reformers, scholars, literary giants, journalists, patriotic orators and scientists, all merging to form the image of a renaissance, and marked the transition from the 'medieval' to the 'modern'.

Bengal played a major role in the Indian independence movement, in which revolutionary groups such as Anushilan Samiti and Jugantar were dominant. Bengalis also played a notable role in the Indian independence movement. Many of the early proponents of the freedom struggle, and subsequent leaders in movement were Bengalis such as Chittaranjan Das, Khwaja Salimullah, Surendranath Banerjea, Huseyn Shaheed Suhrawardy, Netaji Subhash Chandra Bose, Titumir (Sayyid Mir Nisar Ali), Prafulla Chaki, A. K. Fazlul Huq, Maulana Abdul Hamid Khan Bhashani, Bagha Jatin, Khudiram Bose, Surya Sen, Binoy-Badal-Dinesh, Sarojini Naidu, Aurobindo Ghosh, Rashbehari Bose and many more. Some of these leaders, such as Netaji, did not subscribe to the view that non-violent civil disobedience was the best way to achieve Indian Independence, and were instrumental in armed resistance against the British force. Netaji was the co-founder and leader of the Indian National Army (distinct from the army of British India) that challenged British forces in several parts of India. He was also the head of state of a parallel regime, the Arzi Hukumat-e-Azad Hind, that was recognized and supported by the Axis powers. Bengal was also the fostering ground for several prominent revolutionary organisations, the most notable of which was Anushilan Samiti. A large number of Bengalis were martyred in the freedom struggle and many were exiled in Cellular Jail, the much dreaded prison located in Andaman.

Noted Bengali saints, authors, scientists, researchers, thinkers, music composers, painters and film-makers have played a significant role in the development of Bengali culture . The Bengal Renaissance of the 19th and early 20th centuries was brought about after the British introduced Western education and ideas. Among the various Indian cultures, the Bengalis were relatively quick to adapt to the British rule and actually use its principles (such as the judiciary and the legislature) in the subsequent political struggle for independence. The Bengal Renaissance contained the seeds of a nascent political Indian nationalism and was the precursor in many ways to modern Indian artistic and cultural expression.

The Bengali poet and novelist, Rabindranath Tagore, became the first Nobel laureate from Asia when he won the 1913 Nobel

Prize in Literature. Other Bengali Nobel laureates include Amartya Sen (1999 Nobel Memorial Prize in Economic Sciences) and Muhammad Yunus (2006 Nobel Peace Prize). Other famous figures in Bengali literature include Ram Mohan Roy, Kazi Nazrul Islam, and Bangla science fiction writers such as Muhammed Zafar Iqbal, Humayun Ahmed, Jagadananda Roy and Roquia Sakhawat Hussain (Begum Rokeya). Famous Bengali musicians include Ravi Shankar, Sachin Dev Burman, Rahul Dev Burman and Norah Jones; Famous Bengali singers include Kishore Kumar, Heamanta Mukherjee, Manna Dey, Shyamal Mitra, Geeta Dutt, Nachiketa, Shreya Ghoshal, Bappi Lahiri, Abhijeet, Kabir Suman and Rezwana Chowdhury Banya. Famous Bengali scientists include Megh Nad Saha, Prafulla Chandra Roy, Prasanta Chandra Mahalanobis, Amal Kumar Raychaudhuri, Jagadish Chandra Bose and Satyendra Nath Bose; famous Bengali engineers include Fazlur Khan and Amar Bose; famous Bengali filmmakers include Satyajit Ray, Bimal Roy, Mrinal Sen, Ritwik Ghatak, Zahir Raihan, Aparna Sen and Tareque Masud; and famous Bengali entrepreneurs include Sake Dean Mahomed, Amar Bose, Jawed Karim and Subrata Roy .

3

BENGALI LANGUAGE

Bengali or Bangla is an eastern Indo-Aryan language. It is native to the region of eastern South Asia known as Bengal, which comprises present day Bangladesh, the Indian state of West Bengal, and parts of the Indian states of Tripura and Assam. It is written with the Bengali script. With nearly 230 million total speakers, Bengali is one of the most spoken languages (ranking sixth in the world.

Along with other Eastern Indo-Aryan languages, Bengali evolved circa 1000-1200 AD from the Magadhi Prakrit, a declined, vernacular form of the ancient Sanskrit language. It is now the primary language spoken in Bangladesh and is the second most spoken language in India.

With a long and rich literary tradition, Bengali binds together a culturally diverse region and is an important contributor to Bengali nationalism. In Bangladesh, the strong linguistic consciousness led to the Bengali Language Movement, during which on 21 February 1952, several people were killed during protests to maintain the writing of Bengali in the Bengali script and to gain its recognition as a state language of the then Dominion of Pakistan. The day has since been observed as Language Movement Day in Bangladesh, and was declared the International Mother Language Day by UNESCO.

Like other Eastern Indo-Aryan languages, Bengali arose from the eastern Middle Indic languages of the Indian subcontinent. Magadhi Prakrit and Maithili, the earliest recorded spoken languages in the region and the language of the Buddha, evolved into Ardhamagadhi ("Half Magadhi") in the early part of the first millennium CE. Ardhamagadhi, as with all of the Prakrits of North India, began to give way to what are called Apabhramsa languages just before the turn of the first millennium. The local Apabhramsa language of the eastern subcontinent, Purvi Apabhramsa or Apabhramsa Abahatta, eventually evolved into regional dialects, which in turn formed three groups: the Bihari languages, the Oriya languages, and the Bengali-Assamese languages. Some argue that the points of divergence occurred much earlier—going back to even 500 but the language was not static: different varieties coexisted and authors often wrote in multiple dialects. For example, Magadhi Prakrit is believed to have evolved into Apabhramsa Abahatta around the 6th century which competed with Bengali for a period of time.

Usually three periods are identified in the history of Bengali:

Old Bengali (900/1000–1400)—texts include *Charyapada*, devotional songs; emergence of pronouns *Ami, tumi*, etc.; verb inflections *-ila*, *-iba*, etc. Assamese branch out in this period and Oriya just before this period (8th century-1300).

Middle Bengali (1400–1800)—major texts of the period include Chandidas's *Srikrishnakirtan*; elision of word-final *ô* sound; spread of compound verbs; Persian influence. Some scholars further divide this period into early and late middle periods.

New Bengali (since 1800)—shortening of verbs and pronouns, among other changes ("her"; *koriyachhilô korechhilo* he/she had done).

Historically closer to Pali, Bengali saw an increase in Sanskrit influence during the Middle Bengali (Chaitanya era), and also during the Bengal Renaissance. Of the modern Indo-European languages in South Asia, Bengali and Marathi maintain a largely Sanskrit vocabulary base while Hindi and others such as Punjabi, Sindhi and Gujarati are more influenced by Arabic and Persian

Until the 18th century, there was no attempt to document Bengali grammar. The first written Bengali dictionary/grammar, *Vocabolario em idioma Bengalla, e Portuguez dividido em duas partes*, was written by the Portuguese missionary Manoel da Assumpcam between 1734 and 1742 while he was serving in Bhawal. Nathaniel Brassey Halhed, a British grammarian, wrote a modern Bengali grammar (*A Grammar of the Bengal Language (1778)*) that used Bengali types in print for the first time. Raja Ram Mohan Roy, the great Bengali reformer, also wrote a "Grammar of the Bengali Language" (1832).

During this period, the *Choltibhasha* form, using simplified inflections and other changes, was emerging from *Shadhubhasha* (older form) as the form of choice for written Bengali.

Bengali was the focus, in 1951–52, of the Bengali Language Movement (*Bhasha Andolon*) in what was then East Pakistan (now Bangladesh). Although the Bengali language was spoken by the majority of Bangladesh's population, Urdu was legislated as the sole national language. On February 21, 1952, protesting students and activists were fired upon by military and police in Dhaka University and three young students and several other people were killed. Later in 1999, UNESCO decided to celebrate every 21 February as International Mother Language Day in recognition of the deaths of the three students. In a separate event on May 19, 1961, police in Silchar, India, killed eleven people who were protesting legislation that mandated the use of the Assamese language.

Bengali is native to the region of eastern South Asia known as Bengal, which comprises Bangladesh, the Indian state of West Bengal and many parts of Assam. Besides this region it is also spoken by majority of the population in the Indian state of Tripura and in the union territory Andaman and Nicobar Islands. There are also significant Bengali-speaking communities in the

Middle East
Europe
North America
South-East Asia

Regional variation in spoken Bengali constitutes a dialect continuum. Linguist Suniti Kumar Chatterjee grouped these dialects into four large clusters—Rarh, Banga, Kamarupa and Varendra; but many alternative grouping schemes have also been proposed. The south-western dialects (Rarh) form the basis of standard colloquial Bengali, while Bangali is the dominant dialect group in Bangladesh. In the dialects prevalent in much of eastern and south-eastern Bengal (Barisal, Chittagong, Dhaka and Sylhet divisions of Bangladesh), many of the stops and affricates heard in West Bengal are pronounced as fricatives. Western palato-alveolar affricates correspond to eastern . The influence of Tibeto-Burman languages on the phonology of Eastern Bengali is seen through the lack of nasalized vowels. Some variants of Bengali, particularly Chittagonian and Chakma Bengali, have contrastive tone; differences in the pitch of the speaker's voice can distinguish words. Rajbangsi, Kharia Thar and Mal Paharia are closely related to Western Bengali dialects, but are typically classified as separate languages. Similarly, Hajong is considered a separate language, although it shares similarities to Northern Bengali dialects.

During the standardization of Bengali in the late 19th and early 20th century, the cultural center of Bengal was in the city of Kolkata, then Calcutta, founded by the British. What is accepted as the standard form today in both West Bengal and Bangladesh is based on the West-Central dialect of Nadia, an Indian district located on the border of Bangladesh. There are cases where speakers of Standard Bengali in West Bengal will use a different word than a speaker of Standard Bengali in Bangladesh, even though both words are of native Bengali descent. For example, *nun* (salt) in the west corresponds to *lôbon* in the east.

Bengali exhibits diglossia between the written and spoken forms of the language. Two styles of writing, involving somewhat different vocabularies and syntax, have emerged:

Shadhubhasha (*shadhu* = 'chaste' or 'sage'; *bhasha* = 'language') was the written language with longer verb inflections and more of a Sanskrit-derived (*tôtshôm*) vocabulary. Songs such as India's national anthem *Jana Gana Mana* (by Rabindranath Tagore) and national song *Vande Mataram* (by Bankim Chandra Chattopadhyay) were composed in Shadhubhasha. However, use of *Shadhubhasha* in modern writing is negligible, except when it is used deliberately to achieve some effect.

Choltibhasha or *Cholitobhasha* (*cholito* = 'current' or 'running') , known by linguists as *Manno Cholit Bangla* (Standard Colloquial Bengali), is a written Bengali style exhibiting a preponderance of colloquial idiom and shortened verb forms, and is the standard for written Bengali now. This form came into vogue towards the turn of the 19th century, promoted by the writings of Peary Chand Mitra (*Alaler Gharer Dulal,* 1857), Pramatha Chowdhury (*Sabujpatra,* 1914) and in the later writings of Rabindranath Tagore. It is modeled on the dialect spoken in the Shantipur region in Nadia district, West Bengal. This form of Bengali is often referred to as the "Nadia standard" or "Shantipuri bangla".

While most writing is in Standard Colloquial Bengali, spoken dialects exhibit a greater variety. South-eastern West Bengal, including Kolkata, speak in Standard Colloquial Bengali. Other parts of West Bengal and western Bangladesh speak in dialects that are minor variations, such as the Medinipur dialect characterised by some unique words and constructions. However, a majority in Bangladesh speak in dialects notably different from Standard Colloquial Bengali. Some dialects, particularly those of the Chittagong region, bear only a superficial resemblance to Standard Colloquial Bengali. The dialect in the Chattagram region is least widely understood by the general body of Bengalis. The majority of Bengalis are able to communicate in more than one variety—often, speakers are fluent in *cholitobhasha* (Standard Colloquial Bengali) and one or more regional dialects.

Even in Standard Colloquial Bengali, Muslims and Hindu use different words. Due to cultural and religious traditions,

Hindus and Muslims might use, respectively, Sanskrit-derived and Perso-Arabic words. Some examples of lexical alternation between these two forms are:

hello: nômoshkar (S) corresponds to assalamualaikum/slamalikum (A)

invitation: nimontron/nimontonno (S) corresponds to daoat (A)

water : jol (S) corresponds to paani (S)

father : baba (P) corresponds to abbu/abba (A)

(here S = derived from Sanskrit, P = derived from Persian, A = derived from Arabic)

The Bengali writing system is not an alphabetic writing system (e.g. the Latin alphabet), rather an abugida, i.e. its consonant graphemes in general represent a consonant followed by an "inherent" vowel . The script is a variant of the Eastern Nagari script used throughout Bangladesh and eastern India (Assam, West Bengal and the Mithila region of Bihar). The Eastern Nagari script is believed to have evolved from a modified Brahmic script around 1000 CE and is similar to the Devanagari abugida used for Sanskrit and many modern Indic languages (e.g. Hindi, Marathi and Nepali). The Bengali script has particularly close historical relationships with the Assamese script, the Oriya script (although this relationship is not strongly evident in appearance) and Mithilakshar (the native script for Maithili language).

The Bengali script is a cursive script with eleven graphemes or signs denoting nine vowels and two diphthongs, and thirty-nine graphemes representing consonants and other modifiers. There are no distinct upper and lower case letter forms. The letters run from left to right and spaces are used to separate orthographic words. Like Devanagari, Bengali script has a distinctive horizontal line running along the tops of the graphemes that links them together.

Since the Bengali script is an abugida, its consonant graphemes usually do not represent phonetic segments, but carry an "inherent" vowel and thus are syllabic in nature. The inherent vowel is usually a back vowel, either as in "opinion" or , as in [mon] "mind", with variants like the more open . To emphatically represent a consonant sound without any inherent vowel attached to it, a special diacritic, called the *hôshonto* (cf. Arabic *sukun*), may be added below the basic consonant grapheme . This diacritic, however, is not common, and is chiefly employed as a guide to pronunciation. The abugida nature of Bengali consonant graphemes is not consistent, however. Often, syllable-final consonant graphemes, though not marked by a *hôshonto*, may carry no inherent vowel sound .

A consonant sound followed by some vowel sound other than the inherent is orthographically realized by using a variety of vowel allographs above, below, before, after, or around the consonant sign, thus forming the ubiquitous consonant-vowel ligature. These allographs, called *kar*s (cf. Hindi *matra*s) are dependent, diacritical vowel forms and cannot stand on their own. For example, the graph represents the consonant [m] followed by the vowel , where is represented as the diacritical allograph ? (called *i-kar*) and is placed *before* the default consonant sign. combined with seven other vowels and two diphthongs. It should be noted that in these consonant-vowel ligatures, the so-called "inherent" vowel [?] is first expunged from the consonant before adding the vowel, but this intermediate expulsion of the inherent vowel is not indicated in any visual manner on the basic consonant sign ?.

The vowel graphemes in Bengali can take two forms: the independent form found in the basic inventory of the script and the dependent, abridged, allograph form (as discussed above). To represent a vowel in isolation from any preceding or following consonant, the independent form of the vowel is used. For example, in "ladder" and "Hilsa fish", the independent form of the vowel ? is used (cf. the dependent form ?). A vowel at the beginning of a word is always realized using its independent form.

In addition to the inherent-vowel-suppressing *hôshonto*, three more diacritics are commonly used in Bengali. These are the superposed *chôndrobindu* , denoting a suprasegmental for nasalization of vowels "moon"), the postposed *onushshôr* indicating the velar nasal "Bengali") and the postposed *bishôrgo* indicating the voiceless glottal fricative [h] "ouch!") or the gemination of the following consonant

The Bengali consonant clusters are usually realized as ligatures , where the consonant which comes first is put on top of or to the left of the one that immediately follows. In these ligatures, the shapes of the constituent consonant signs are often contracted and sometimes even distorted beyond recognition. In Bengali writing system, there are nearly 285 such ligatures denoting consonant clusters. Although there exist a few visual formulas to construct some of these ligatures, many of them have to be learned by rote. Recently, in a bid to lessen this burden on young learners, efforts have been made by educational institutions in the two main Bengali-speaking regions (West Bengal and Bangladesh) to address the opaque nature of many consonant clusters, and as a result, modern Bengali textbooks are beginning to contain more and more "transparent" graphical forms of consonant clusters, in which the constituent consonants of a cluster are readily apparent from the graphical form. However, since this change is not as widespread and is not being followed as uniformly in the rest of the Bengali printed literature, today's Bengali-learning children will possibly have to learn to recognize both the new "transparent" and the old "opaque" forms, which ultimately amounts to an increase in learning burden.

Bengali punctuation marks, apart from the downstroke *dari* (|), the Bengali equivalent of a full stop, have been adopted from western scripts and their usage is similar.

Whereas in western scripts (Latin, Cyrillic, etc.) the letter-forms stand on an invisible baseline, the Bengali letter-forms hang from a visible horizontal headstroke called the *matra* (not to be confused with its Hindi cognate *matra*, which denotes the dependent forms of Hindi vowels). The presence and absence of this *matra* can be important. For example, the letter and the numeral ? "3" are distinguishable only by the presence or absence of the *matra,* as is the case between the consonant cluster and the independent vowel . The letter-forms also employ the concepts of letter-width and letter-height (the vertical space between the visible *matra* and an invisible baseline).

There is yet to be a uniform standard collating sequence (sorting order) of Bengali graphemes. Experts in both India and Bangladesh are currently working towards a common solution for this problem.

The Bengali script, with a few small modifications, is also used for writing Assamese. Other related languages in the region also make use of the Bengali alphabet. Meitei, a Sino-Tibetan language used in the Indian state of Manipur, has been written in the Bengali abugida for centuries, though Meitei Mayek (the Meitei abugida) has been promoted in recent times. The Bengali script has been adopted for writing the Sylheti language as well, replacing the use of the old Sylheti Nagori script.

Romanization

Several conventions exist for writing Indic languages including Bengali in the Latin script, including "International Alphabet of Sanskrit Transliteration" or IAST (based on diacritics), "Indian languages Transliteration" or ITRANS (uses upper case alphabets suited for ASCII keyboards), and the National Library at Calcutta romanization.

In the context of Bangla Romanization, it is important to distinguish transliteration from transcription. Transliteration is orthographically accurate (i.e. the original spelling can be recovered), whereas transcription is phonetically accurate (the pronunciation can be reproduced). Since English does not have the sounds of Bangla, and since pronunciation does not completely reflect the spellings, being faithful to both is not possible.

Although it might be desirable to use a transliteration scheme where the original Bangla orthography is recoverable from the

Latin text, Bangla words are currently Romanized on Wikipedia using a phonemic transcription, where the pronunciation is represented with no reference to how it is written.

Magadhan languages such as Bengali are known for their wide variety of diphthongs, or combinations of vowels occurring within the same syllable. Several vowel combinations can be considered true monosyllabic diphthongs, made up of the main vowel (the **nucleus**) and the trailing vowel (the **off-glide**). Almost all other vowel combinations are possible, but only across two adjacent syllables, such as the disyllabic vowel combination *kua* "well". As many as 25 vowel combinations can be found, but some of the more recent combinations have not passed through the stage between two syllables and a diphthongal monosyllable. There are nineteen diphthongs in Bangal language.

In standard Bengali, stress is predominantly initial. Bengali words are virtually all trochaic; the primary stress falls on the initial syllable of the word, while secondary stress often falls on all odd-numbered syllables thereafter, giving strings such as ***shô**-ho-**jo**-gi-**ta*** "cooperation", where the boldface represents primary and secondary stress. The first syllable carries the greatest stress, with the third carrying a somewhat weaker stress, and all following odd-numbered syllables carrying very weak stress. However in words borrowed from Sanskrit, the root syllable is stressed, causing them to be out of harmony with native Bengali words.

Adding prefixes to a word typically shifts the stress to the left. For example, while the word ***shob**-bho* "civilized" carries the primary stress on the first syllable [shob], adding the negative prefix creates ***ô**-shob-bho* "uncivilized", where the primary stress is now on the newly added first syllable . In any case, word-stress does not alter the meaning of a word and is always subsidiary to sentence-stress.

For Bengali words, intonation or pitch of voice has minor significance, apart from a few isolated cases. However in sentences intonation does play a significant role. In a simple declarative sentence, most words and/or phrases in Bengali carry a rising tone, with the exception of the last word in the sentence, which only carries a low tone. This intonational pattern creates a musical tone to the typical Bengali sentence. This intonation with low and high tones alternating until the final drop in pitch to mark the end of the sentence.

In sentences involving focused words and/or phrases, the rising tones only last until the focused word; all following words carry a low tone. This intonation pattern extends to wh-questions, as wh-words are normally considered to be focused. In yes-no questions, the rising tones may be more exaggerated, and most importantly, the final syllable of the final word in the sentence takes a high falling tone instead of a flat low tone.

Vowel length is not contrastive in Bengali; all else equal, there is no meaningful distinction between a "short vowel" and a "long vowel", unlike the situation in many other Indic languages. However, when morpheme boundaries come into play, vowel length can sometimes distinguish otherwise homophonous words. This is due to the fact that open monosyllables (i.e. words that are made up of only one syllable, with that syllable ending in the main vowel and not a consonant) have somewhat longer vowels than other syllable types. For example, the vowel in *cha:* "tea" is somewhat longer than the first vowel in *chata* "licking", as *cha:* is a word with only one syllable, and no final consonant. (The long vowel is marked with a colon : in these examples.) The suffix *ta* "the" can be added to *cha:* to form *cha:ta* "the tea". Even when another morpheme is attached to *cha:*, the long vowel is preserved. Knowing this fact, some interesting cases of apparent vowel length distinction can be found. In general Bengali vowels tend to stay away from extreme vowel articulation.

Furthermore, using a form of reduplication called "echo reduplication", the long vowel in *cha:* can be copied into the reduplicant *ta:*, giving *cha:ta:* "tea and all that comes with it". Thus, in addition to *cha:ta* "the tea" (long first vowel) and *chata* "licking" (no long vowels), we have *cha:ta:* "tea and all that comes with it"

4

BENGALI LITERATURE

Bengali literature is literary works written in Bengali language particularly from Bangladesh and the Indian provinces of West Bengal and Tripura. The history of Bengali literature traces back hundreds of years while it is impossible to separate the literary trends of the two Bengals during the pre-independence period. Post independent Bangladesh has given birth to its own distinct set of literature.

The first evidence of Kamrupi literature is known as Charyapada or Chari-Siddha-Pada in dedication on the names of four sons of Brahma, a collection of 8th-12th century CE Buddhist mystic poems from eastern India or ancient Kingdom of Kamarupa now read as Kamrup that provides early examples of Assamese, Oriya and Bengali languages. Poets of these Charyapadas, the Siddhas belonged to the various regions of ancient Kamarupa kingdom or present Assam, Bengal, Orissa and Bihar. Charyapada is also the oldest known written form of Kamrupi.

The famous Bengali linguist Harprashad Shastri discovered the palm leaf Charyapada manuscript in the Nepal Royal Court Library in 1907.

In the middle of 19th century, Bengali literature gained momentum. During this period, the Bengali *Pandits* of Fort William College did the tedious work of translating the text books in Bengali to help teach the British some Indian languages including Bengali. This work played a role in the background in the evolution of Bengali prose. In 1814, Raja Ram Mohan Roy arrived in Calcutta and engaged in literary pursuits. Translating from Sanskrit to Bengali, writing essays on religious topics and publishing magazines were some the areas he focussed on. He established a cultural group in the name of 'Atmiya Sabha' (Club of Kins) in 1815. Another significant contributor of Bengali literature in its early stage was Ishwar Chandra Bandyopadhyaya.

In 1857, the famous 'Sipahi Bidroha' (Sepoy Mutiny) took place. With the wind of it, 'Nil Bidroho' (Indigo Revolt) scattered all over then Bengal region. This Nil Bidroha lasted for more than a year (In 1859-1860). The literature world was shaken with this revolt. In the light of this revolt, a great drama was published from Dhaka in the name of 'Neel Dorpon' (The Indigo Mirror). Dinabandhu Mitra was the writer of this play.

In this time, Michael Madhusudan Dutt emerged as the first epic-poet of modern bangla literature. Dutt, a Christian by conversion, is best known for his Ramayana-based masterpiece, "The Slaying of Meghnadh," (in Bengali "*Meghnadh Bodh Kabbo*" , which essentially follows in the poetic tradition of Milton's *Paradise Lost*. Those who have read it consider this work a world-class epic poem of the modern era. Michael Madhusudan Dutta is also credited with the introduction of sonnets to Bangla literature. He ruled the Bangla literature world for more than a decade (1858-1863). Dutt can also be credited to be a pioneer of the blank verse in Bengali literature. His style was deemed as "Amitrakhar Chhanda".

Bankim Chandra Chattopadhyay starts his journey through bangla literature with his first published novel 'Durgeshnondini' (Daughter of the Fort Lord) in 1865. He is considered as one of the leading Bengali novelists and is popularly known as the author of India's first *national song*, "Bande Matarom" (pronounced in Hindi "Vande Mataram"). The song appears in his novel "Anandamath", considered to be a masterpiece in Bengali literature.

Others

Bangla literature also become rich with its variations. It started to spread its different branches also. in poetry Ishwar Chandra Gupta, Biharilal Chakravarty, Kaykobad, in novel Romesh Chunder Dutt, Mir Mosharraf Hossain, in plays Girish Chandra Ghosh, in essays Akshay Kumar Boral, Ramendra Sundar Tribedi and many others contributed to enrich bangla literature in this time.

A lot of literature magazines and newspapers started to come under day light. A number of educational institutes appears all over the region. This helps a lot to nurture the future author and poets of bangla language.

Pre-Tagore era also saw an undercurrent of popular literature which was based on daily lifestyle of contemporary Bengal. The prose style as well as the humour in these stories were often crass & blunt. A masterpiece in this regard was "Hutom Pechar Naksha" (The sketch of Owl) written by Kaliprasanna Singha. It depicts a witty & vivid desciption of the "Babu" culture in 19th century Kolkata. Other notable mentions in this regard are "Alaler Ghorer Dulal" (The spoilt brat) by Pyarichand Mitra, "Ramtanu Lahiri o tatkalin Banga shamaj" (Ramtanu Lahiri & contemporary Bengali society) by Nyaymohan Tarkalankar, "Naba Babu Bilas" & "Nana Bibi Bilas" by Bhabanicharan Bandopadhyay. These books arguably portrayed contemporary Bengali dialect & society promptly, along with the now extinct music genres of Khisti, Kheur & Kabiyal gaan by stalwarts like Rupchand Pakhi, Bhola Moyra. Books like these will become rarer once Tagore's restarined & cultured approach impressed the Bengali society.

Possibly the most prolific writer in Bangla is Nobel laureate Rabindranath Tagore. Tagore dominated both the Bengali and Indian philosophical and literary scene for decades. His 2,000 *Rabindrasangeets* play a pivotal part in defining Bengali culture, both in West Bengal and Bangladesh. He is the author of the national anthems of both India and Bangladesh, both composed in Bangla. Other notable Bangla works of his are *Gitanjali*, a book of poems for which he was awarded the Nobel Prize for Literature in 1913, and many short stories and a few novels. It is widely accepted that Bangla Literature accomplished its contemporary look by the writings and influence of Rabindranath..

In a similar category is Kazi Nazrul Islam, who was invited to post-partition Bangladesh as the National Poet and whose work transcends sectarian boundaries. Adored by Bengalis both in Bangladesh and West Bengal, his work includes 3,000 songs, known as both as *nazrul geeti* and "nazrul sangeet". He is frequently called the rebel poet mainly because of his most famous and electrifying poem "Bidrohi" or "The Rebel", and also because of his strong sympathy and support for revolutionary activities leading to India's independence from British Rule. His songs and poems were frequently used during the Bangladesh Liberation War as well. Though he is acknowledged as the rebel poet, Nazrul very effectively contributed in all branches of literature. He wrote poems that light the fire against inequality or injustice and at the same time is known for his poignant romantic poems as well. He wrote a lot of Islami Ghazals and in the same time wrote a number of *Shyama Sangeet* (songs for the Hindu Mother Goddess, Kali). Nazrul was not only a poet, he was writer, musician, journalist and philosopher. He was sent to jail for his literary works against the then prevailing British rule.

Sarat Chandra Chattopadhyay was one of the most popular novelists of early 20th century whose speciality was exploring life and sufferings of women in contemporary rural Bengal. His sympathy towards the common rural folks in "pallisamaj" and a trademark simplified Bengali as a writing style made him one of the most popular writer in his time. Even long after his death many Bengali and Bollywood blockbusters were based on his novels. After him Tarashankar Bandopadhyay, Bibhutibhushan Bandopadhyay, Manik Bandopadhyay, are the three Bandopadhyays who broke out into a new era of realistic writing style. Where the two of the above Bibhutibhusan and Manik had long standing influence on the two of the most brilliant film directors from Bengal, Satyajit Ray and Ritwik Ghatak respectively. Other famous bengali novelists are Jagadish Gupta, Satinath Bhaduri, Balai Chand Mukhopadhyay (Banophool), Saradindu Bandopadhyay, Kamal Kumar Majumdar, Sunil Gangopadhyay, Sandipan Chattopadhyay, Shumotho Nath Ghosh, Gagendra Kumar Mitra, Bimal Mitra, Bimal Kar, Samaresh Basu, Mani Shankar Mukherjee (Shankar), etc. Seeds of bengali science fiction could be observed in the writings of Jagadish Chandra Bose, which was later put into a definite genre by writers such as Jagadananda Roy, Hemlal Dutta, Begum Roquia Sakhawat Hussain, Premendra Mitra, Satyajit Ray. Where Satyajit Ray is also notable for his short stories where he revives the tradition of Thakurmar Jhuli into a mixture of fantasy, mystery, science, and fairy tale.

The genre of parallel novel-writing started from the 1960s with the Hungryalist Movement. Malay Roy Choudhury, Subimal Basak and Basudeb Dasgupta are known to be the most experimental novelists belonging to this movement. Basudeb is known to his readers for his only novel Kheladhula. Malay is famous for his Dubjaley trilogy and Subimal for his broken narrative CHHATAMATHA.

More experimental novelists who came into the scene in the midst of surging change in Bengali Literature are: Udayan Ghosh, Rabindra Guha, Kamal Chakraborty, Barin Ghoshal, Subimal Mishra, Arupratan Basu, Nabarun Bhattacharya.

In the New Age (21st Century), Arupratan Ghosh can be considered the only novelist of this genre with his novel Suryaheen (published in 2007).

Bengali literature is also famous for short stories. Some of the famous short story writers are Rabindranath Tagore, Manik Bandopadhyay, Jagadish Gupta, Tarashankar Bandopadhyay, Bibhuti Bhushan Bandopadhyay, Rajshekhar Basu (Parasuram), Premendra Mitra, Kamal Kumar Majumdar, Shibram Chakrabarti, Saradindu Bandopadhyay, Subodh Ghosh,

Narendranath Mitra, Jyotirindra Nandi, Bimal Kar, Narayan Gangopadhyay, Shumotho Nath Ghosh, Gagendra Kumar Mitra, Santosh Ghosh, Debesh Roy, Anish Deb, Abhijnan Roychowdhury, Satyajit Roy, Lila Majumder, Shiresendu Mukhopaddhyay, Ratan Lal Basu, Sayed Walliullaha, Sandipan Chattopadhyay, Basudeb Dasgupta, Subimal Mishra, Arupratan Basu, Kamal Chakraborty, Aboni Dhar, Nabarun Bhattacharya, Akhtaruzzaman Ilias, Dipak Barua, Mahmudul Huq, Hasan Azizul Huq, etc. Malay Roy Choudhury has introduced a completely new genre of Bengali short story writing called 'Atibastab' or 'Hyperreal' during 1990s.

New writers and experimental short stories (apart from the mainstream ones) were not in the scene over the last two decades (1980's and 90's). A revival of new experimental short stories is observed in the New Age (21st Century). Pratishedhak, a New Age magazine (which first revived the experimental short story culture in early 2000), has played a major influential role to promote further revival of the experimental short story writing culture. Some New Age short story writers are:

Souptik Chakraborty, Arko Chattopadhyay, Arupratan Ghosh, Sudeshna Majumdar and Ratul Paul.

The first New Age short story book - Napoleoner Nabobarsho by Souptik Chakraborty - was published in 2008.

Jatindramohan Bagchi, Kazi Nazrul Islam, Jibanananda Das, along with Buddhadeva Bose, marks the beginning of the major move to transcend the Tagore legacy . Even though Jibanananda went through a terbulent and difficult financial troubles and met an unfortunate accident caliming his life early in his writing career, he remains to be the most influential poet of post-Rabindranath era. The new genre of Bengali poets departed considerably from Tagore's ideological style and adopted various themes and philosophies such as Marxism , Freudian interpretation of mind, which were avoided and often criticized by Rabindranath Tagore. These three marked the beginning of the era that will burst with activities and urge to merge with the greater world of poetry absorbing elements from them. Commonly called polli-kobi (*pastoral poet*) Jasimuddin, Shamsur Rahman, widely known for his 'playing with words' are also notable.

There has been only one pathbreaking literary movement in West Bengal, namely The Hungry generation or Hungryalism. The famous poets of this movement are Malay Roy Choudhury, Shakti Chattopadhyay, Benoy Majumdar, Samir Roychoudhury, Falguni Ray, Saileswar Ghose, Pradip Chowdhuri, Subo Acharya, Arunesh Ghose, Tridib Mitra and Debi Ray. The fiction writers are Sandipan Chattopadhyay, Basudeb Dasgupta, Subimal Basak, Malay Roy Choudhury and Samir Roychoudhury. The painters are Anil Karanjai and Karunanidhan Mukhopadhyay.

Prakalpana Movement

Prakalpana Movement, branded by Steve LeBlanc, the noted US critic, as 'a tiny literary revolution', 'nurtured' by Kolkata, has been fostering its new genres of Prakalpana fiction, Sarbangin poetry and Chetanavyasism for over four decades, spearheaded by Vattacharja Chandan, beginning in 1969. It is probably the only bilingual (Bengali -English) literary movement in India mothered by Bengali literature, that has spread its wings world wide through the participation of well known international avant-garde writers and mail artists such as Richard Kostelanetz, John M. Bennett, Sheila Murphy, Don Webb, John Light, Carla Bertola &c, with notable Bengali poets, writers and artists like Vattacharja Chandan, Dilip Gupta, Asish Deb, Bablu Roy Choudhury, Syamoli Mukherjee Bhattacharjee, Boudhayan Mukhopadhyay, Ramratan mukhopadhyay, Nikhil Bhaumik, Utpal, Abhijit Ghosh, Arun Kumar Chakraborty, Niva De etc.

Since the mid 80's Bengali Literature experienced a new genre of Bengali poetry called New Poetry. From the early 90's a Kolkata based poetry journal Kabita Campus has organized various workshops and poetry-camps focusing on this genre.

In 2003 some poets of that journal have separately started another one named Natun Kabita containing their ideas and poems, through both online and print media. Another new age poetry magazine in the same sphere is Boikhoribhashya. Poets associated with this literary movement are:

Barin Ghosal, Ranjan Maitra, Swapan Roy, Dhiman Chakraborty, Alok Biswas, Pronob Pal, Soumitra Sengupta, Arupratan Ghosh, Indranil Ghosh, Amitava Praharaj and Debanjan Das.

Rajarshi Chattopadhyay, Atanu Bandopadhyay, Pradip Chakraborty are the poets who joined this movement in mid 90's.

The first decade of this century (2000 - 09) is considered to be the period of a *New Age* of Bengali poetry.

Prominent poets rising from the period are:

Sankha Subhra Devbarman, Arindam Ray, Arup Ghosh, Tanmay Mandal, Arjun Bandopadhyay, Susnata Jana, Himalay Jana, Kaushik Bhowmik, Pallab Chakrabarti, Sanghamitra Haldar, Himadri Mukhopadhyay, Somnath Ghosal, Swagata Dasgupta, Nabendu Bikash Ray, Ripon Fio, Atanu Sinha, Sandip Kumar, Paramita Das .

Seminal Hindu religious works in Bangla include the many songs of Ramprasad Sen. His works (still sung today) from the 17th century cover an astonishing range of emotional responses to the goddess Kali, detailing complex philosophical statements based on Vedanta teachings and more visceral pronouncements of his love of the goddess. They are known as *Shyama Sangeet* and were the literary inspiration for Kazi Nazrul Islam's later, famed Shyama Sangeet. There are also the laudatory accounts of the lives and teachings of the Vaishnava saint Chaitanya Mahaprabhu (the *Choitanyo Choritamrit*) and Shri Ramakrishna (the *Ramakrishna Kathamrita,* translated roughly as Gospel of Ramakrishna). There is also a large body of Islamic literature, that can be traced back at least to *Noornama* by Abdul Hakim. *Bishad Sindhu* depicting the death of Hussain in Karbala is very popular novel written by Mir Mosharraf Hossain. Later works influenced by Islam include devotional songs written by Nazrul, and popularized by Abbas Uddin, among others.

Bauls and traditional singers

The mystic Bauls of the Bengal countryside who preached the boundless spiritual truth of *Sôhoj Pôth* (the Simple, Natural Path) and *Moner Manush* (The Man of The Heart) drew on Vedantic philosophy to propound transcendental truths in song format, traveling from village to village proclaiming that there was no such thing as Hindu, Muslim or Christian, only *moner manush.*

The literature discussed so far can be more or less regarded as the common heritage of both Bangladesh and West Bengal. Since the partition of Bengal in 1947, the east and west parts of Bengal have also developed their own distinctive literatures. For example, the Naxalite movement has influenced much of West Bengal's literature, whereas the Liberation War has had a similarly profound impact on Bangladeshi literature.

Major literary figures in Bangladesh

Shawkat Osman, Ahsan Habib, Abul Hossain, Farrukh Ahmed, Syed Ali Ahsan, Shamsur Rahman, Syed Shamsul Haque, Al Mahmud, Abu Zafar Obaidullah, Sufia Kamal, Al Mahmud, Abubakar Siddique, Ghulam Murshid, Hasan Azizul Huq, Selina Hossain, Arunabh Sarkar, Shawkat Ali, Akhtaruzzaman Ilias, Rafiq Azad, Nirmalendu Goon, Mahadev Saha, Abul Hasan, Humayun Azad, Abid Azad, Sikdar Aminul Haq, Shaheedul Jahir, Humayun Ahmed, Imdadul Haque Milon, Anisul Hoque, Hasan Hafizur Rahman, Abu Hena Mustafa Kamal, Shaheed Quaderi, Abu Hasan Shahriar, Khondakar Ashraf Hossain, Hassanal Abdullah, Rahman Henry, Dipak Barua, Helal Hafiz, Azeezul Haq, Omar Ali, and to name a few.

Major literary figures in West Bengal

Nihar Ranjan Gupta, Ashutosh Mukhopadhyay, Sunil Gangopadhyay, Nabaneeta Dev Sen, Syed Mustafa Siraj, Baren Gangopadhyay, Shirshendu Mukhopadhyay, Amiya Bhushan Mazumdar, Lokenath Bhattacharya, Debesh Roy, Atin Bandyopadhyay, Shankha Ghosh, Sandipan Chattopadhyay, Samir Roychoudhury, Subimal Basak, Shakti Chattopadhyay, Mahasweta Devi, Moti Nandi, Kamal Kumar Majumdar, Subimal Mishra, Shankar, Suchitra Bhattacharya, Vattacharja Chandan, Bani Basu, Buddhadeb Guha, Shiersendu Mukhopaddhyay, Suchitra Bhattacharya, Pranabkumar Chattopadhyay, etc.

Literay figures since 1970's (Parallel or non Main-stream Genre)

Swadesh Sen, Barin Ghosal, Pranabkumar Chattopadhayay, Biplab Majee, Ananya Roy, Subimal Mishra, Vattacharja Chandan, Kamal Chakraborty, Ranjan Maitra, Swapan Roy, Shankar Lahiri, Dhiman Chakraborty, Anirban Mukhopadhyay, Aryanil Mukhopadhyay, Sarthak Roychowdhury, Sharmi Pandey, Shubhankar Das, Rajarshi Chattopadhyay, Arupratan Ghosh, Indranil Ghosh, Amitava Praharaj, Souptik Chakraborty, Animikh Patra, Paramita Das, Himadri Mukhopadhyay, Arindam Ray, Anamitra Roy, Tanmay Mandal, Deb Maity, Swagata Dasgupta, Kaushik Bhowmik, Debanjan Das, Arjun Bandopadhyay, Souva Chattopadhyay, Atanu Sinha, Arup Ghosh.

Charyapada is the oldest known Bengali written form. It is actually collection of poems. It was written on 9th century and Harprashad Sastri discovered in the Nepal Royal Court Library in 1907. It is a palm leaf manuscript. Charyapada's language is referred to as Alo-Andhari (light and shadow), meaning *twi-light language*. The manuscript has 47 verses, written by 23 po-ets, probably lived between the 9th and 11th centuries AD. And came from the various regions of Bengal, Orissa, Assam and

Bihar. Some poets were Sarhapa, shabar pa, Luipa, Dombipa, Bhusukupa, kahnapa, Kukkuripa, Minapa, Aryadev, Dhendhanpa.

A torn manuscript of the Sreekrishna Kirtana Kabya was discovered by Basanta Ranjan Roy Biddyadwallav in 1909 from the house of Debendranath Chatterjee at a village named kakinla in the district of Bankura [West Bengal]. Shreekrishna Kirtana Kabya was composed by Boru Chandidas. While, Charyapada shows us the most ancient example of Bengali language, Shreekrishna Kirtana depicts a new kind of speech style very clearly. According to Suniti Kumar Chatterjee, "The Grammar of the speech of the Shreekrishna Kirtana gives a clue to many of the forms of New Bengali"

The Chaitanya Charitamrita is the magnum-opus of the Bengali saint/author Krishna Dasa Kaviraja (1496-? CE). The book, a hybrid Bengali and Sanskrit biography, documents the life and precepts of the Vaishnava saint Chaitanya Mahaprabhu (1486–1533), who is considered by his followers to be an incarnation of Radha and Krishna combined. Chaitanya is a pivotal figure of the Hindu sect Gaudiya Vaishnavism.

As a religious text, the Chaitanya Charitamrita is the main theological resource for Gaudiya Vaishnava Theology and is divided into three sections, Adi-lila, Madhya-lila and Antya-lila.

The Hungryalist movement, better known as Hungry generation was launched from the Patna residence of Malay Roy Choudhury in November 1961 by Malay along with Shakti Chattopadhyay, Samir Roychoudhury and Haradhon Dhara alias Debi Roy. Later around 30 more poets, writers and painters joined the movement. In view of their anti-establishment writings, some of them were arrested in 1964, and ultimately charges were framed against Malay Roy Choudhury for his poem Stark Electric Jesus. He was jailed by the lower court, though the High Court exonerated him. The police action resulted into disbanding of the movement in 1965. However, the movement had a lasting effect, inasmuch as the writing trend changed, and subsequently there was a little magazine explosion.

Major changes occurred in the Bengali Literature centering the Little Magazine Movement in the 1970s, with Kaurab - as the hub. Kaurab is a literary & cultural magazine which is about four decades old. Prime cult-figures of Kaurab are Swadesh Sen, Kamal Chakraborty, Barin Ghosal, Shankar Lahiri, Shankar Chakraborty and Aryanil Mukhopadhyay.

Since the mid 80's Bengali Literature experienced a new genre of Bengali poetry called New Poetry. From the early 90's with impetus from a Kolkata based poetry journal Kabita Campus, New Poetry has begun to gain immense acclamation from young contemporary poets of Bengal. In 2003 some poets of this genre have started a journal named Natun Kabita containing their ideas and poems, through, both, online and print media. Another new age poetry magazine in the same sphere is Boikhoribhashya. Poets associated with this literary movement are:

Barin Ghosal, Ranjan Maitra, Swapan Roy, Dhiman Chakraborty, Alok Biswas, Pronob Pal, Saumitra Sengupta, Arupratan Ghosh, Indranil Ghosh, Amitava Praharaj and Debanjan Das.

Rajarshi Chattopadhyay, Atanu Bandopadhyay, Pradip Chakraborty are the poets who joined this movement in the mid 90's.

In West Bengal the first decade of this century (2000–09) is considered to be the period of a New Age Little Magazine Movement. The magazines prominent in this period are:

Sanjhbati, Lalon, Bodhshabda, Pratishedhak, Abosardanga, Ashtray, Ahir , Byas, Thek , etc.

Major figures rising from the period are:

Aritra Sanyal, Animikh Patra, Souptik Chakraborty, Arjun Bandopadhyay, Somtirtha Nandi, Susnata Jana, Himalay Jana, Kaushik Bhowmik, Arindam Ray, Tanmay Mandal, Anamitra Roy, Rohon Kuddus, Sanghamitra Haldar, Himadri

Mukhopadhyay, Somnath Ghosal, Swadesh Misra, Swagata Dasgupta, Nabendu Bikash Ray, Arko Chattopadhyay, Ripon Fio, Atanu Sinha, Sayantan Mukhopadhyay, Paramita das, Souva Chattopadhyay, Deb Maity, Saibal Sarkar, Arup Ghosh , Koel Mitra.

There is a Little Magazine Library and Research Centre at Tamer Lane (run by Sandip Dutta since 1978), Kolkata, India which collects Bengali little magazines published from anywhere in the world.

The region of Bengal is one of the most densely populated regions on earth, with a population density exceeding 900/km^2. Most of the Bengal region lies in the low-lying Ganges–Brahmaputra River Delta or Ganges Delta, the world's largest delta. In the southern part of the delta lies the Sundarbans—the world's largest mangrove forest and home of the Bengal tiger. Though the population of the region is mostly rural and agrarian, two megacities, Kolkata (previously Calcutta) and Dhaka (previously Dacca), are located in Bengal. The Bengal region is renowned for its rich literary and cultural heritage as well as its immense contribution to the socio-cultural uplift of Indian society in the form of the Bengal Renaissance, and revolutionary activities during the Indian independence movement.

The exact origin of the word *Bangla* or Bengal is unknown, though it is believed to be derived from the Dravidian-speaking tribe *Bang* that settled in the area around the year 1000 BC.

Other accounts speculate that the name is derived from *Vanga* , which came from the Austric word "Bonga" meaning the Sun-god. The word *Vanga* and other words speculated to refer to Bengal (such as Anga) can be found in ancient Indian texts including the Vedas, Jaina texts, the Mahabharata and Puranas. The earliest reference to "Vangala" has been traced in the Nesari plates (805 AD) of Rashtrakuta Govinda III which speak of Dharmapala as the king of Vangala.

Some accounts claim that the word may derive from bhang, a preparation of cannabis which is used in some religious ceremonies in Bengal. Dravidians migrated to Bengal from the south, while Tibeto-Burman peoples migrated from the Himalayas, followed by the Indo-Aryans from north-western India. The modern Bengali people are a blend of these people. Smaller numbers of Pathans, Persians, Arabs and Turks also migrated to the region in the late Middle Ages while spreading Islam.

Remnants of Copper Age settlements in the Bengal region date back 4,300 years, . After the arrival of Indo-Aryans, the kingdoms of Anga, Vanga and Magadha were formed by the 10th century BC, located in the Bihar and Bengal regions. Magadha was one of the four main kingdoms of India at the time of Buddha and consisted of several Janapadas. One of the earliest foreign references to Bengal is the mention of a land named Gangaridai by the Greeks around 100 BC, located in an area in Bengal. From the 3rd to the 6th centuries CE, the kingdom of Magadha served as the seat of the Gupta Empire.

The first recorded independent king of Bengal was Shashanka, reigning around early 7th century. After a period of anarchy, the native Buddhist-Hindu Pala Empire ruled the region for four hundred years, and expanded across much of the Indian subcontinent into Afghanistan during the reigns of Dharmapala and Devapala. The Pala dynasty was followed by a shorter reign of the Hindu Saiva Sena dynasty. Islam was introduced to Bengal by Arab Muslim traders. A large number of people became Muslims in the twelfth century through Sufi missionaries. Subsequent Muslim conquests helped spread Islam throughout the region. Bakhtiar Khilji, a Turkic general of the Slave dynasty of Delhi Sultanate, defeated Lakshman Sen of the Sena dynasty and conquered large parts of Bengal. Consequently, the region was ruled by dynasties of sultans and feudal lords under the Delhi Sultanate for the next few hundred years. In the sixteenth century, Mughal general Islam Khan conquered Bengal. Susequently, Afghan ruler Sher Shah Suri and Hindu king Hemu had ruled for shorter periods. However, administration by governors appointed by the court of the Mughal

Empire gave way to semi-independence of the area under the Nawabs of Murshidabad, who nominally respected the sovereignty of the Mughals in Delhi. The most notable among them is Murshid Quli Khan, who was succeeded by Alivardi Khan.

Portuguese traders arrived late in the fifteenth century, once Vasco da Gama reached India by sea in 1498. European influence grew until the British East India Company gained taxation rights in Bengal *subah,* or province, following the Battle of Plassey in 1757, when Siraj ud-Daulah, the last independent Nawab, was defeated by the British. The Bengal Presidency was established by 1766, eventually including all British territories north of the Central Provinces (now Madhya Pradesh), from the mouths of the Ganges and the Brahmaputra to the Himalayas and the Punjab. The Bengal famine of 1770 claimed millions of lives. Calcutta was named the capital of British India in 1772. The Bengal Renaissance and Brahmo Samaj socio-cultural reform movements had great impact on the cultural and economic life of Bengal. The failed Indian rebellion of 1857 started near Calcutta and resulted in transfer of authority to the British Crown, administered by the Viceroy of India. Between 1905 and 1911, an abortive attempt was made to divide the province of Bengal into two zones .

Bengal has played a major role in the Indian independence movement, in which revolutionary groups were dominant. Armed attempts to overthrow the British Raj reached a climax when Subhash Chandra Bose led the Indian National Army against the British. Bengal was also central in the rising political awareness of the Muslim population—the Muslim League was established in Dhaka in 1906. In spite of a last ditch effort to form a United Bengal, when India gained independence in 1947, Bengal was partitioned along religious lines. The western part went to India (and was named West Bengal) while the eastern part joined Pakistan as a province called East Bengal (later renamed East Pakistan, giving rise to Bangladesh in 1971). The circumstances of partition was bloody, with widespread religious riots in Bengal.

The post-partition political history of East and West Bengal diverged for the most part. Starting from the Bengali Language Movement of 1952. political dissent against West Pakistani domination grew steadily. Awami League, led by Sheikh Mujibur Rahman, emerged as the political voice of the Bengali-speaking population of East Pakistan by 1960s. In 1971, the crisis deepened when Rahman was arrested and a sustained military assault was launched on East Pakistan. Most of the Awami League leaders fled and set up a government-in-exile in West Bengal. The guerrilla Mukti Bahini and Bengali regulars eventually received support from the Indian Armed Forces in December 1971, resulting in a decisive victory over Pakistan on 16 December in the Bangladesh Liberation War or Indo-Pakistani War of 1971. The post independence history of Bangladesh was strife with conflict, with a long history of political assassinations and coups before parliamentary democracy was established in 1991. Since then, the political environment has been relatively stable.

West Bengal, the western part of Bengal, became a state in India. In the 1960s and 1970s, severe power shortages, strikes and a violent Marxist-Naxalite movement damaged much of the state's infrastructure, leading to a period of economic stagnation. The Bangladesh Liberation War of 1971 resulted in the influx of millions of refugees to West Bengal, causing significant strains on its infrastructure.[27] West Bengal politics underwent a major change when the Left Front won the 1977 assembly election, defeating the incumbent Indian National Congress. The Left Front, led by Communist Party of India (Marxist) (CPI(M)) has governed for the last three decades. The state's economic recovery gathered momentum after economic reforms in India were introduced in the mid-1990s by the central government, aided by election of a new reformist Chief Minister Buddhadeb Bhattacharya in 2000.

About 250 million people live in Bengal, around 68% of them in Bangladesh and the remainder in West Bengal. The population density in the area is more than 900/km^2; making it among the most densely populated areas in the world.

Bengali is the main language spoken in Bengal. English is often used for official work. There are small minorities who speak Hindi, Urdu, Chakma. There are several tribal languages including Santhali. Nepali is spoken primarily by the Gorkhas of Darjeeling district of West Bengal.

66% of the total Bengali population is Muslim, and 33% is Hindu. In Bangladesh 89.7% of the population is Muslim and 9.2% are Hindus (Bangladesh Census 2001). In West Bengal, Hindus are the majority with 72.5% of the population while Muslims comprise 25%, and other religions make up the remainder. Other religious groups include Buddhists, Christians, and Animists. About 2% of the population is tribal.

Life expectancy is around 63 years, and are almost same for the men and women. In terms of literacy, West Bengal leads with 69.22% literacy rate, in Bangladesh the rate is approximately 41%. The level of poverty is high, the proportion of people living below the poverty line is more than 30%.

About 20,000 people live on chars. Chars are temporary islands formed by the deposition of sediments eroded off the banks of the Ganges in West Bengal which often disappear in the monsoon season. They are made of very fertile soil. The inhabitants of chars are not recognised by the Government of West Bengal on the grounds that it is not known whether they are Bengalis or Bangladeshi refugees. Consequently, no identification documents are issued to char-dwellers who cannot benefit from health care, barely survive due to very poor sanitation and are prevented from emigrating to the mainland to find jobs when they have turned 14. On a particular char it was reported that 13% of women died at childbirth.

Agriculture is the leading occupation in the region. Rice is the staple food crop. Other food crops are pulses, potato, maize, and oil seeds. Jute is the principal cash crop. Tea is also produced commercially; the region is well known for Darjeeling and other high quality teas. The service sector is the largest contributor to the gross domestic product of West Bengal, contributing 51% of the state domestic product compared to 27%

from agriculture and 22% from industry. State industries are localized in the Kolkata region and the mineral-rich western highlands. Durgapur–Asansol colliery belt is home to a number of major steel plants. West Bengal has the third largest economy (2003–2004) in India, with a net state domestic product of US$ 21.5 billion. During 2001–2002, the state's average SDP was more than 7.8%—outperforming the National GDP Growth. The state has promoted foreign direct investment, which has mostly come in the software and electronics fields; Kolkata is becoming a major hub for the Information technology (IT) industry. Owing to the boom in Kolkata's and the overall state's economy, West Bengal is now the third fastest growing economy in the country.

Since 1990, Bangladesh has achieved an average annual growth rate of 5% according to the World Bank, despite the hurdles. The middle class and the consumer industry have seen some growth. Bangladesh has seen a sharp increase in foreign direct investment. A number of multinational corporations, including Unocal Corporation and Tata, have made major investments, the natural gas sector being a priority. In December 2005, the Central Bank of Bangladesh projected GDP growth around 6.5%. Although two-thirds of Bangladeshis are farmers, more than three quarters of Bangladesh's export earnings come from the garment industry, which began attracting foreign investors in the 1980s due to cheap labour and low conversion cost. In 2002, the industry exported US$5 billion worth of products. The industry now employs more than 3 million workers, 90% of whom are women. A large part of foreign currency earnings also comes from the remittances sent by expatriates living in other countries.

One significant contributor to the development of the economy of Bangladesh has been the widespread propagation of microcredit by Grameen Bank (founded by Muhammad Yunus) and other similar organizations. Together, these organizations had about 5 million members by late 1990s.

The common Bengali language and culture anchors the shared tradition of two parts of politically divided Bengal. Bengal has a long tradition in folk literature, evidenced by the *Charyapada, Mangalkavya, Shreekrishna Kirtana, Maimansingha Gitika* or *Thakurmar Jhuli*. Bengali literature in the medieval age was often either religious (e.g. Chandidas), or adaptations from other languages (e.g. Alaol). During the Bengal Renaissance of the nineteenth and twentieth centuries, Bengali literature was modernized through the works of authors such as Michael Madhusudan Dutta, Bankim Chandra Chattopadhyay, Rabindranath Tagore and Kazi Nazrul Islam.

Rabindranath Tagore reshaped Bengali literature and music in the late 19th and early 20th centuries. He is Asia's first Nobel laureate and composer of Jana Gana Mana the national anthem of India as well as Amar Shonar Bangla the national anthem of Bangladesh.

Kazi Nazrul Islam was a revolutionary Bengali poet who led the Bengal Renaissance in Muslim majority areas of Bengal. He is the national poet of Bangladesh.

The Baul tradition is a unique heritage of Bangla folk music. The scholar saint Sri Anirvan loved Baul music, and in fact described himself as a simple Baul. Other folk music forms include Gombhira, Bhatiali and Bhawaiya. Folk music in Bengal is often accompanied by the ektara, a one-stringed instrument. Other instruments include the dotara, dhol, flute, and tabla. The region also has an active heritage in North Indian classical music.

Bengal had also been the harbinger of modernism in Indian arts. Abanindranath Tagore, one of the important 18th century artist from Bengal is often referred to as the father of Indian modern art. He had established the first non-British art academy in India known as the Kalabhavan within the premises of Santiniketan. Santiniketan in course of time had produced many important Indian artists like Gaganendranath Tagore, Nandalal Bose, Jamini Roy, Benode Bihari Mukherjee and Ramkinkar Baij.

In the post-independence era, Bengal had produced important artists like Somenath Hore, Meera Mukherjee and Ganesh Paine.

Rice and fish are traditional favorite foods, leading to a saying that in Bengali, *mach ar bhaath bangali baanaay*, that translates as "fish and rice make a Bengali". Bengal's vast repertoire of fish-based dishes includes Hilsa preparations, a favorite among Bengalis. Bengalis make distinctive sweetmeats from milk products, including *Rôshogolla, Chômchôm*, and several kinds of *Pithe*.

Bengali women commonly wear the *shari* and the salwar kameez, often distinctly designed according to local cultural customs. In urban areas, many women and men wear Western-style attire. Among men, European dressing has greater acceptance. Men also wear traditional costumes such as the *panjabi* with *dhuti* or *pyjama*, often on religious occasions. The lungi, a kind of long skirt, is widely worn by Bangladeshi men.

The greatest religious festivals are the two Eids (Eid ul-Fitr and Eid ul-Adha) for the Muslims, and the autumnal Durga Puja for Hindus. Christmas (called *Bôrodin* (Great day) in Bangla), Buddha Purnima are other major religious festivals. Other festivities include Pohela Baishakh (the Bengali New Year), Basanta-Utsab, Nobanno, and *Poush parbon* (festival of Poush).

Bengali cinema are made both in Kolkata and Dhaka. The Kolkata film industry is older and particularly well known for its art films. Its long tradition of film making has produced world famous directors like Satyajit Ray, while contemporary directors include Buddhadev Dasgupta and Aparna Sen. Dhaka also has a vibrant commercial industry and more recently has been home to critically acclaimed directors like Tareque Masud. Mainstream Hindi films of Bollywood are also quite popular in both West Bengal and Bangladesh. Around 200 dailies are published in Bangladesh, along with more than 1800 periodicals. West Bengal had 559 published newspapers in 2005, of which 430 were in Bangla. Cricket and football are popular sports in the Bengal region. Local games include sports such as Kho Kho and Kabaddi, the later being the national sport of Bangladesh. An Indo-Bangladesh *Bangla Games* has been organized among the athletes of the Bengali speaking areas of the two countries.

Geographic, cultural, historic, and commercial ties are growing, and both countries recognize the importance of good relations. During and immediately after Bangladesh's struggle for independence from Pakistan in 1971, India assisted refugees from East Pakistan, and intervened militarily to help bring about the independence of Bangladesh. The Indo-Bangladesh border length of 4,095 km (2,545 mi), West Bengal has a border length of 2,216 km (1,377 mi). Despite overlapping historic, geographic and cultural ties, the relation between West Bengal and Bangladesh is still well below the potential. The pan-Bengali sentiment among the people of the two parts of Bengal was at its height during the 1971 Bangladesh Liberation War. While the government radio and national press in India might have backed the struggle out of strategic considerations, the Bengali broadcast and print media went out of its way to lend overwhelming support.

Frequent air services link Kolkata with Dhaka and Chittagong. A bus service between Kolkata and Dhaka is operational. The primary road link is the Jessore Road which crosses the border at Petrapole-Benapole about 175 km northwest of Kolkata. The Train service between Kolkata and Dhaka, which was stopped after the Indo-Pakistani War of 1965, was resumed in 2008.

Visa services are provided by Bangladesh's consulate at Kolkata's Bangabandhu Sheikh Mujibur Rahman Road and India's high commissions in Dhaka, Chittagong and Rajshahi. India has a liberal visa policy and nearly 500,000 visas are issued every year to Bangladeshi students, tourists, health-tourists and others who visit West Bengal and often transit to other parts of India. West Bengalis visit Bangladesh for limited numbers of tourism, pilgrimage, trade, expatriate assignments; there is significant potential for growth as Bangladesh's stability, economy, moderation in religion and tourist infrastructure improves. In addition West Bengal hosts the celebrated and controversial Bangladeshi author Taslima Nasreen.

Undocumented immigration of Bangladeshi workers is a controversial issue championed by right-wing nationalist parties in India but finds little sympathy in West Bengal. India has fenced the border to control this flow but immigration is still continuing. A rallying cry for the right-wing Hindu parties in India is that the demographics changed such as in West Bengal's border district of Malda from Hindu-majority to Muslim-majority.

The official land border crossing at Petrapole-Benapole is the primary conduit for the over $1 billion trade between the two halves of Bengal. The volume of unofficial exports to Bangladesh from India is reportedly in the range of $350–500 million each year. Bangladesh argues with merit that India needs to open up its border more to Bangladeshi exports. Other landports between the two Bengals are Changrabandha-Burimari and Balurghat-Hili.

Cultural exchanges between the two parts of Bengal have been somewhat (but not fully) impacted by ups and downs in India-Bangladesh relations and in the influence of extremist Islamist groups in Bangladesh. West Bengal singers and actors complained about being rejected visas in previous years. Bangladesh television channels are widely watched in West Bengal. West Bengal media have an audience in Bangladesh. In foreign countries such as the U.S., Canada, UK, and UAE, it is common for Bengalis from both sides to form joint cultural associations and friendships, although inter-marriage is not significant, especially across religious barriers.

5

EARLY LIFE OF RABINDRANATH TAGORE

The first four decades in the life of Rabindranath Tagore (1861–1941) were formative of both his artistic and much of his political thinking. He was a Bengali poet, Brahmo philosopher, and scholar.

Tagore was born at No. 6 Dwarkanath Tagore Lane, Jorasanko — the address of his family mansion. In turn, Jorasanko was located in the Bengali section of north Kolkata , located near Chitpur Road. The area immediately around the Jorasanko Tagore mansion was rife with poverty and prostitution. He was the son of Debendranath Tagore(1817–1905) and Sarada Devi (1830–1875). Debendranath Tagore had formulated the Brahmo faith propagated by his friend, the reformer Raja Ram Mohan Roy. Debendranath became the central figure in Brahmo society after Ray's death, who was addressed out of respect by followers as *maharishi*. He continued to lead the *Adi Brahmo Shomaj* until he died. Women who married into Tagore's clan were generally from the villages of East Bengal (now Bangladesh).

Tagore was born the youngest of fourteen children. As a child, Tagore lived amidst an atmosphere where literary magazines were published, musical recitals were held, and theatre performed. The Jorasanko Tagores were indeed at the center of a large and art-loving social group. Tagore's oldest brother, Dwijendranath, was a respected philosopher and poet. Another brother, Satyendranath, was the first ethnically Indian member appointed to the elite and formerly all-white Indian Civil Service. Yet another brother, Jyotirindranath Tagore, was a talented musician, composer, and playwright. Among his sisters, Swarnakumari Devi earned fame as a novelist in her own right. Jyotirindranath's wife, Kadambari — who was slightly older than Tagore — was a dear friend and a powerful influence on Tagore. Her abrupt suicide in 1884 left him distraught for years, and left a profound mark on the emotional timbre of Tagore's literary life.

Tagore — nicknamed "Rabi" — was born the youngest of fourteen children. As part of the Jorasanko branch of the Tagore family, Tagore grew up exposed to the publication of literary magazines, in-home musical recitals, and theatrical performances. Tagore was also influenced by older brothers Dwijendranath (a philosopher), Satyendranath (the first Indian appointed to the elite Indian Civil Service), and Jyotirindranath (a musician, composer, and playwright). His female relatives included sister Swarna Kumari Devi (a novelist) and Kadambari (Jyotirindranath's wife, whose 1884 suicide burdened Tagore for years).

For the first decade or so of his life, Tagore remained distant from his father, who was frequently away touring northern India, England, and other places. Meanwhile, Tagore was mostly confined to the family compound — he was forbidden to leave it for any purpose other than traveling to school. He thereby grew increasingly restless for the outside world, open spaces, and nature. On the other hand, Tagore was intimidated by the mansion's perceived ghostly and enigmatic aura. Further, Tagore was ordered about the house by servants in a period he would later designate as a "servocracy". Incidents included servants dunking the heads of Tagore and his siblings into drinking water held by giant clay cisterns — used as a means to quiet the children. In addition, Tagore often refused food to satisfy servants, was confined to a chalk circle by the second-in-command servant named Shyam in parody of an analogous forest trial that Sita underwent in the *Ramayana*, and was told horrific stories telling the bloody exploits of outlaw dacoits.

Tagore was also tutored at home by Hemendranath, his brother. While being physically conditioned — for example, swimming in the Ganges River, taking long treks through hilly areas, and practicing judo and wrestling — he was also given Bengali-language lessons in anatomy, drawing, English language (Tagore's least favorite subject), geography, gymnastics, history, literature, mathematics, and Sanskrit imparted before and after school. Meanwhile, Tagore was developed an aversion towards formal learning and schooling, stating later that the role of teaching was not to explain things, but rather to

> "knock at the doors of the mind. If any boy is asked to give an account of what is awakened in him by such knocking, he will probably say something silly. For what happens within is much bigger than what comes out in words. Those who pin their faith on university examinations as the test of education take no account of this."

Tagore started writing poems around age eight, and he was urged by an older brother to recite these to people in the mansion — including to an impressed Brahmo nationalist, newspaper editor, and Hindu Mela organizer. At age eleven, Tagore underwent the *upanayan* coming-of-age rite: he and two relatives were shaved bald and sent into retreat, where they were to chant and meditate. Tagore instead rollicked, beating drums and pulling his brothers' ears, after which he received a sacred thread of investiture. Afterward, on February 14, 1873, Tagore experienced the first close contact with his father when they set out together from Calcutta on a months-long tour of India. They first made for Shantiniketan ("Abode of Peace"), a family estate acquired in 1863 by Debendranath composed of two rooms set amidst a mango grove, trees, and plants. Tagore later recalled his stay among the rice paddies:

> "What I could not see did not take me long to get over — what I did see was quite enough. There was no servant rule, and the only ring which encircled me was the blue of the horizon, drawn around these [rural] solitudes by their presiding goddess. Within this I was free to move about as I chose."

After several weeks, they traveled to Amritsar, staying near the Harmandir Sahib and worshipping at a Sikh gurudwara. They also read English- and Sanskrit-language books, exposing Tagore to astronomy, biographies of such figures as Benjamin Franklin, and Edward Gibbon's *The History of the Decline and Fall of the Roman Empire*. Later, in mid-April, Tagore and his father set off for the remote and frigid Himalayan hill station of Dalhousie, India, near what is now Himachal Pradesh's border with Kashmir. There, at an elevation of some 2,300 meters (7,500 feet), they lived in a house high atop Bakrota hill. Tagore was taken aback by the region's deep gorges, alpine forests, and mossy streams and waterfalls. Yet Tagore was also made to study lessons — including such things as Sanskrit declensions — starting in the icy pre-dawn twilight. Tagore took a break from his readings for a noontime meal; thereafter, Tagore was to continue his studies, although Tagore was often allowed to fall asleep. Some two months later, Tagore left his father in Dalhousie and journeyed back to Calcutta.

In early October 1878, Tagore traveled to England with the intent of becoming a barrister. He first stayed for some months at a house that the Tagore family owned near Brighton and Hove, in Medina Villas; there, he attended a Brighton school (not, as has been claimed, Brighton College — his name does not appear in its admissions register). In 1877, his nephew and niece — Suren and Indira, the children of Tagore's brother Satyendranath — were sent together with their mother (Tagore's sister-in-law) to live with him. Later, after spending

Christmas of 1878 with his family, Tagore was escorted by his elder brother's friend to London; there, Tagore's relatives hoped that he would focus more on his studies. He enrolled at University College London. However, he never did complete his degree, leaving England after just over a year's stay. This exposure to English culture and language would later percolate into his earlier acquaintance with Bengali musical tradition, allowing him to create new modes of music, poetry, and drama. Nevertheless, Tagore neither fully embraced English strictures nor his family's traditionally strict Hindu religious observances in either his life or in his art, choosing instead to pick the best from both realms of experience.

In 1890, Tagore began managing his family's estates in Shelaidaha, a region now in Bangladesh; he was joined by his wife and children in 1898. Tagore, known then as "Zamindar Babu", often traveled dozens of miles across the vast estate while living out of the *Padma*, the family's converted flat-bottomed keel-less barge (known as a "budgerow" or a *Daccai bajras*). His dealings with his tenants included the annual collection of (mostly token) rents and the blessing of villagers; in exchange for his generosity, villagers regularly held feasts in Tagore's honour — these featured such fare as dried rice and sour milk. In this decade, Tagore authored many works and founded a new genre of Bengali writing: the short story. Tagore wrote some fifty-nine of them in 1891–1901; many had ironic elements or had emotional appeal while they dealt with a wide range of Bengali lifestyles. Examples include *Sonar Tari* (1894), *Chitra* (1896), and *Katha O Kahini* (1900); his essays, poems, and plays of the time also touched on village life.

6

WORKS OF RABINDRANATH TAGORE

The Works of Rabindranath Tagore consist of poems, novels, short stories, dramas, paintings, drawings, and music that Bengali poet and Brahmo philosopher Rabindranath Tagore created over his lifetime.

Tagore's literary reputation is disproportionately influenced by regard for his poetry; however, he also wrote novels, essays, short stories, travelogues, dramas, and thousands of songs. Of Tagore's prose, his short stories are perhaps most highly regarded; indeed, he is credited with originating the Bangla-language version of the genre. His works are frequently noted for their rhythmic, optimistic, and lyrical nature. However, such stories mostly borrow from deceptively simple subject matter — the lives of ordinary people.

Dramas

Tagore's experiences with drama began when he was sixteen, when he played the lead role in his brother Jyotirindranath's adaptation of Molière's *Le Bourgeois Gentilhomme*. Tagore wrote his first original dramatic piece when he was twenty — *Valmiki Pratibha* ("The Genius of Valmiki"), which was shown at the Tagores' mansion. His works — emphasizing fusion of lyrical flow and emotional rhythm tightly focused on a core idea — were unlike previous Bengali drama. Tagore stated that his works sought to articulate "the play of feeling and not of action". In 1890 he wrote *Visarjan* ("Sacrifice"); it has been regarded as his finest drama. In the original Bangla language, such works included intricate subplots and extended monologues. Later, Tagore's dramas used more philosophical and allegorical themes. For example, his 1912 *Dakghar* ("Post Office") received rave reviews in Europe and was shown in London (at the Irish Theater), Berlin, and Paris. Lastly, Tagore's *Chandalika* ("Untouchable Girl") was modeled on an ancient Buddhist legend describing how Gautama Buddha's disciple Ananda asks water of an *Ȧdivasi* (tribal girl, probably of the numerous Santal tribes found throughout western regions of Bengal.

Tagore's plays also are important to Bengali literature. All of his plays have been repeatedly staged and re-interpreted over the years. His most famous play, perhaps, is *Raktakaravi* ("Red Oleanders") — the name of a red flower. It tells of a king who lives behind an iron curtain while his subjects have cruelty and death delivered upon them at the slightest pretext. People are forced to work in the mines so that the kleptocratic king and his cronies may render themselves even more wealthy. The play follows the heroine Nandini, who leads the people and finally the king himself towards the destruction of this artifact of subjugation. However, this ultimate victory is preceded by numerous deaths, most importantly that of Ranjan, Nandini's lover, and Kishore a young boy devoted to her. Tagore devoted much effort to *Raktakaravi*, with (at least) eleven extant revisions. However, Tagore's motivation in writing *Raktakaravi* is disputed, with some suggesting negative opinions formed during his visit to the mines of Bombay. Others attribute it to dislike of the West, while others think that a woman motivated him to create Nandini. Tagore's other notable plays include *Chitrangada, Raja, Valmiki-Pratibha,* and *Mayar Khela*.

Tagore began his career in short stories in 1877 — when he was only sixteen — with "Bhikharini" ("The Beggar Woman").

With this, Tagore effectively invented the Bangla-language short story genre. The four years from 1891 to 1895 are known as Tagore's "Sadhana" period (named for one of Tagore's magazines). This period was among Tagore's most fecund, yielding more than half the stories contained in the three-volume *Galpaguchchha*, which itself is a collection of eighty-four stories. Such stories usually showcase Tagore's reflections upon his surroundings, on modern and fashionable ideas, and on interesting mind puzzles (which Tagore was fond of testing his intellect with). Tagore typically associated his earliest stories (such as those of the "*Sadhana*" period) with an exhuberance of vitality and spontaneity; these characteristics were intimately connected with Tagore's life in the common villages of, among others, Patisar, Shajadpur, and Shilaida while managing the Tagore family's vast landholdings. There, he beheld the lives of India's poor and common people; Tagore thereby took to examining their lives with a penetrative depth and feeling that was singular in Indian literature up to that point. In particular, such stories as "Cabuliwallah" ("The Fruitseller from Kabul", published in 1892), "Kshudita Pashan" ("The Hungry Stones") (August 1895), and "Atithi" ("The Runaway", 1895) typified this analytic focus on the downtrodden. In "The Fruitseller from Kabul", Tagore speaks in first person as town-dweller and novelist who chances upon the Afghani seller. He attempts to distill the sense of longing felt by those long trapped in the mundane and hardscrabble confines of Indian urban life, giving play to dreams of a different existence in the distant and wild mountains: "There were autumn mornings, the time of year when kings of old went forth to conquest; and I, never stirring from my little corner in Calcutta, would let my mind wander over the whole world. At the very name of another country, my heart would go out to it ... I would fall to weaving a network of dreams: the mountains, the glens, the forest .... ". Many of the other "Galpaguchchha" stories were written in Tagore's *Sabuj Patra* period (1914–1917, again, named after one of the magazines that Tagore edited and heavily contributed to).

Tagore's *Golpoguchchho* ("Bunch of Stories") remains among the most popular fictional works in Bangla literature. Its continuing influence on Bengali art and culture cannot be overstated; to this day, *Golpoguchchho* remains a point of cultural reference. *Golpoguchchho* has furnished subject matter for numerous successful films and theatrical plays, and its characters are among the most well known to Bengalis. The acclaimed film director Satyajit Ray based his film *Charulata* ("The Lonely Wife") on *Nastanirh* ("The Broken Nest").

This famous story has an autobiographical element to it, modelled to some extent on the relationship between Tagore and his sister-in-law, Kadambari Devi. Ray has also made memorable films of other stories from *Golpoguchchho*, including *Samapti, Postmaster* and *Monihara*, bundling them together as *Teen Kanya* ("Three Daughters"). *Atithi* is another poignantly lyrical Tagore story which was made into a film of the same name by another noted Indian film director Tapan Sinha. Tarapada, a young Brahmin boy, catches a boat ride with a village zamindar. It turns out that he has run away from his home and has been wandering around ever since. The zamindar adopts him, and finally arranges a marriage to his own daughter. The night before the wedding Tarapada runs away again. Strir Patra (The letter from the wife) has to be one of the earliest depictions in Bangla literature of such bold emancipation of women. Mrinal is the wife of a typical Bengali middle class man. The letter, written while she is traveling (which constitutes the whole story), describes her petty life and struggles. She finally declares that she will not return to his patriarchical home, stating *Amio bachbo. Ei bachlum* ("And I shall live. Here, I live").

In *Haimanti,* Tagore takes on the institution of Hindu marriage. He describes, via *Strir Patra,* the dismal lifelessness of Bengali women after they are married off, hypocrisies plaguing the Indian middle class, and how Haimanti, a sensitive young woman, must — due to her sensitiveness and free spirit — sacrifice her life. In the last passage, Tagore directly attacks the Hindu custom of glorifying Sita's attempted self-immolation as a means of appeasing her husband Rama's doubts (as depicted in the epic Ramayana). Tagore also examines Hindu-Muslim tensions in *Musalmani Didi,* which in many ways embodies the essence of Tagore's humanism. On the other hand, *Darpaharan* exhibits Tagore's self-consciousness, describing a young man harboring literary ambitions. Though he loves his wife, he wishes to stifle her literary career, deeming it unfeminine. Tagore himself, in his youth, seems to have harbored similar ideas about women. *Darpaharan* depicts the final humbling of the man via his acceptance of his wife's talents. As with many other Tagore stories, *Jibito o Mrito* provides the Bengalis with one of their more widely used epigrams: *Kadombini moriya proman korilo she more nai* ("Kadombini died, thereby proved that she hadn't").

Among Tagore's works, his novels are among the least-acknowledged. These include *Chaturanga, Gora* (1910), *Shesher Kobita, Ghare Baire, Char Odhay,* and *Noukadubi. Ghare Baire* or *The Home and the World,* (which was also released as the film by Satyajit Ray, *Ghare Baire*) examines rising nationalistic feeling among Indians while warning of its dangers, clearly displaying Tagore's distrust of nationalism — especially when associated with a religious element. In some sense, *Gora* shares the same theme, raising questions regarding the Indian identity. As with *Ghore Baire,* matters of self-identity, personal freedom, and religious belief are developed in the context of an involving family story and a love triangle.

Shesher Kobita (translated twice, as *Last Poem* and as *Farewell Song*) is his most lyrical novel, containing as it does poems and rhythmic passages written by the main character (a poet). Nevertheless, it is also Tagore's most satirical novel, exhibiting post-modernist elements whereby several characters make gleeful attacks on the reputation of an old, outmoded, oppressively-renowned poet (named Rabindranath Tagore).

Though his novels remain under-appreciated, they have recently been given new attention through many movie adaptations by such film directors as Satyajit Ray, Tapan Sinha and

Tarun Majumdar. The recent among these is a version of *Chokher Bali* directed by Rituparno Ghosh, which features Aishwariya Rai. A favorite trope of these directors is to employ *rabindra sangeet* in the film adaptations' soundtracks.

Among Tagore's notable non-fiction books are *Iurop Jatrir Patro* ("Letters from Europe") and *Manusher Dhormo* ("The Religion of Man").

Free-verse translation by Tagore (*Gitanjali*, verse VII):

"My song has put off her adornments. She has no pride of dress and decoration. Ornaments would mar our union; they would come between thee and me; their jingling would drown thy whispers."

"My poet's vanity dies in shame before thy sight. O master poet, I have sat down at thy feet. Only let me make my life simple and straight, like a flute of reed for thee to fill with music."

Besides *Gitanjali*, other notable works include *Manasi*, *Sonar Tori* ("Golden Boat"), *Balaka* ("Wild Geese" — the title being a metaphor for migrating souls), and *Purobi*. *Sonar Tori*'s most famous poem — dealing with the ephemeral nature of life and achievement — goes by the same name; it ends with the haunting phrase (*"shunya nadir tire rahinu pari / jaha chhilo loye gelo shonar tori"* — "all I had achieved was carried off on the golden boat — only I was left behind."). In *Dui Bigha Jomi* ("A Strip of Land"), Tagore explores the plight of a sharecropper whose meager parcel of farmland is taken over — using falsified papers — by a moneylender; the poem concludes: *"rajar hosto kore shomosto kangaler dhon churi"* ("it is the king's hand that steals from the downtrodden"). *Sonar Tori* also contains *Hing Ting Chhot*. Although comic in form, it illuminates what Tagore saw as Bengali society's crippling lack of vision, originality, and wisdom: *durbodh ja chhilo kichu hoye gelo jol, shunno akasher moto ottonto nirmol* ("Oh yes, now all has been explained, like the empty expanse of the open sky"). Throughout his life, Tagore experimented with different poetic styles. For example, in his early years, he occasionally wrote his works in *Shadhu Bhasha* (a Sanskritized dialect of Bangla); later, Tagore moved seamlessly to using *Chalit* (a more popular dialect). Lastly, the poems in *Balaka* mark the start of an epoch; the most notable of these reads:

Ore nabin, ore amaar kaNcha,
ore shobujh, ore abhujh,
aadh marader ga mere tui bancha.
Oh youth, oh the tender,
oh green, oh unknowing,
hit the bodies of the halfdead to bring them back to life.

Later, with the development of new poetic ideas in Bengal — many originating from younger poets seeking to break with Tagore's style — Tagore absorbed new poetic concepts, which allowed him to further develop a unique identity. Examples of this include *Africa* and *Camalia,* which are among the better known of his latter poems.

Fig 6.1 *Dancing Girl", an undated ink-on-paper piece by Tagore.*

Music and Artwork

Tagore was also an accomplished musician and painter. Indeed, he wrote some 2,230 songs; together, these comprise *rabindra sangeet*, now an integral part of Bengali culture. Yet, Tagore's music is inseparable from his literature, most of which — poems or parts of novels, stories, or plays alike — became lyrics for his songs. These ran the gamut of human emotion, and are still frequently used to give voice to a wide range of experiences. Such is true of two such works: Bangladesh's *Aamaar Sonaar Baanglaa* and India's *Jana Gana Mana*; Tagore thus became the only person ever to have written the national anthems of two nations. Tagore also had an artist's eye for his own handwriting, embellishing the cross-outs and word layouts in his manuscripts with simple artistic leitmotifs.

At age sixty, Tagore took up drawing and painting; successful exhibitions of his many works — which made a debut appearance in Paris upon encouragement by artists he met in the south of France — were held throughout Europe. Tagore — who likely exhibited protanopia ("color blindness"), or partial lack of (red-green, in Tagore's case) colour discernment — painted in a style characterised by peculiarities in aesthetic and colouring style. Nevertheless, Tagore took to emulating numerous styles, including that of craftwork by the Malanggan people of northern New Ireland, Haida carvings from the Pacific Northwest region of North America, and woodcuts by Max Pechstein.

7

RABINDRA SANGEET

Rabindra Sangeet , also known as Tagore Songs in English, is a form of music composed by Rabindranath Tagore who added a new dimension to the musical concept of India in general and Bengal in specific.

Rabindra Sangeet use Indian classical music and traditional folk music as sources. Tagore wrote some 2,230 songs.

Rabindra Sangeet has had a very strong influence in bengali cultural. These songs are regarded as cultural treasures of Bengal in both Bangladesh and West Bengal (India).

The *Rabindrasangeet,* which deal with varied themes are immensely popular and form a foundation for the Bengali ethos that is comparable to, perhaps even greater than, that which Shakespeare has on the English-speaking world. It is said that his songs are the outcome of 500 years of literary & cultural churning that the Bengali community has gone through.

In his book *Caste and Outcaste,* Dhan Gopal Mukerji has said that these songs transcend the mundane to the aesthetic and express all ranges and categories of human emotion. The poet had given a voice to all—big or small, rich or poor. The poorest boatman on the Ganges as well as the rich landlord find expression for their emotional trials and tribulations in Tagore's songs.

Rabindrasangeet has evolved into a distinctive school of music. Practitioners of this genre are known to be fiercely protective of tradionalist practice. Novel interpretations and variations have drawn severe censure in both West Bengal and Bangladesh. And like Beethoven's symphonies or Vilayat Khan's sitar, Rabindrasangeet demands an educated, intelligent & cultured audience to appreciate the lyrical beauty of his compositions.

He was among the first to recognize that cinema should have its own language. In 1929 he wrote, "The beauty and grandeur of this form in motion has to be developed in such a way that it becomes self-sufficient without the use of words." The inherent beauty & depth of Tagore's songs have persuaded a number of filmmakers to use Tagore's songs in their films including Satyajit Ray, Ritwik Ghatak, Mrinal Sen, Nitin Bose, Tapan Sinha and Kumar Shahani.His songs were also used in British, European & Australian movies just to capture the mood of a cinematic situation & to reveal a delicate interplay of relationships. Similarly, Hollywood film Siddhartha (1972) had Tagore's "O Nadi Re" sung by Hemant Kumar.

Ritwik Ghatak said of Tagore, "That man has culled all my feelings from long before my birth…I read him and find that...I have nothing new to say." In his *Meghe Dhaka Tara* (The Cloud-capped Star) and *Subarnarekha*, Ghatak uses *Rabindrasangeet* to express the poignancy of post-Partition Bengal.

Two of the songs written by Tagore are the national anthems of India and Bangladesh. These are:

Uniqueness of Rabindrasangeet

Tagore died in 1941, but his sublimity and effect of his songs are eternal. In his songs, pure poetry has integrated the creator, nature and love. Human love (Prem) transforms into love and devotion for the creator (Bhakti). The collection of his 2000 odd songs is known as Gitabitan (garden of songs). The four major parts of this book are Puja (worship), Prem (love), Prakriti (Nature) and Bichitra (Diverse). However, the categorizations melt away in many songs. A song about rains may reveal longing for the lover. A love song may turn out to be love of the creator. Here are first two lines of one song:

Tagore died in 1941, but his sublimity and effect of his songs are eternal. In his songs, pure poetry has integrated the creator, nature and love. Human love (Prem) transforms into love and devotion for the creator (Bhakti). The collection of his 2000 odd songs is known as Gitabitan (garden of songs). The four major parts of this book are Puja (worship), Prem (love), Prakriti (Nature) and Bichitra (Diverse). However, the categorizations melt away in many songs. A song about rains may reveal longing for the lover. A love song may turn out to be love of the creator.

Singers of Rabindrasangeet

Some of the well-known singers of *Rabindrasangeet* are:

Ashoketaru Bandyopadhyay

Kanika Bandyopadhyay: her original name was "Anima" but Tagore had renamed her "Kanika" and Abanindranath Tagore used to call her *Mohar* by which name she is known to many of her dedicated listeners.

Debabrata Biswas: also known as the *Second Man* of Rabindrasangeet and the most popular male voice.

Suman Chatterjee
Chinmoy Chattopadhyay
Rezwana Chowdury Bonya
Sreya Guhathakurta
Arundhuti Home Chowduri
Purba Dam
Swagatalakshmi Dasgupta
Rajeswari Dutta
Banani Ghosh

Santidev Ghosh: direct disciple of Rabindranath Tagore and Dinendranath Tagore.

Namita Ghoshal
Swapna Ghoshal

Rono Gohathakurota
Ritu Guha
Gita Ghatak
Jayeeta Ghosh
Kishore Kumar
Rama Mondal
Pijush Kanti Sarkar

Suchitra Mitra: like Kanika Bandyopadhyay, Suchitra is another female pioneer and virtuoso of Rabindra Sangeet. Many of the contemporary singers are disciples of Suchitra and Kanika.

Dwijen Mukhopadhyay Purabi Mukhopadhyay: Purabi Mukhopadhyay is an exponent of Rabindra Sangeet. She is a direct disciple of Debabrata Biswas. Hemanta Kumar Mukhopadhyay: although he sang Bengali contemporary and Hindi songs also, Rabindrasangeet was his passion. He was among those who were instrumental in making Rabindrasangeet popular across all strata of Bengali population. Pankaj Mullick: also known as the *First Man* of Rabindrasangeet. Sushil Mullick Rajasree Subinoy Roy Arghya Sen Nilima Sen: she was the Principal of Sangeet Bhavan and Swastika Mukhopadhyay was her student,who now teaches Rabindra Sangeet there. Indranil Sen Subhomita Bandyopadhyay Lopamudra Mitra Sinjini Acharya Mazumdar Arundhati Vinod Deshmukh .

Teachers of Rabindrasangeet

India

Some of the well-known teachers of Rabindrasangeet (barring Tagore himself) are:

Dinendra Nath Tagore
Shantideb Ghosh
Ashoketaru Bandyopadhyay
Dwijen Mukhopadhay
Shailaja Ranjan Majumdar

Maya Sen
Purabi Mukhopadhyay
Ruma Guha Thakurta
Suchitra Mitra
Kanika Bandyopadhyay
Subinoy Roy
Nilima Sen

Bangladesh

In Bangladesh, prominent Rabindrasangeet trainers who have contributed immensely in developing new artistes include:

Abdul Ahad Deceased
Sanjida Khatun
Wahidul Haq Deceased
Kalim Sarafi
Ajit Ray
Anisur Rahman
Papia Sarwar
Rezwana Chowdhury Banya]
Abdul Wadud
Suman Chowdhury
Mujubul Quayyum
Dodul Ahmed
Kaderi Kibria
Rokaiya Hasina

8

TAGORE'S GARDEN OF EDEN

Some places about whose geographical location there cannot be even a grain of doubt, somehow gain mythical status in public imagination. To those who have read Rabindranath Tagore's autobiographical writings — *Jiban Smriti* and *Chhelebela* — Penetir Bagaan or a garden house in Panihati, is much more than a real garden near Sodepur. It is like Eden.

The Sodepur crossing of BT Road is busy even at 10pm. On its left is a rickshaw stand, beside which is a police kiosk, and adjacent to it is a narrow road that snakes all the way to the river bank. On both sides are dwelling houses, one uglier than the other, and ponds, one of which has been turned into a swimming pool. Most old houses are falling to pieces. At what seems the end of the road is a large gate with the words Govinda Kumar Home painted on it with white. As in most old places, ancient houses have either disappeared or else they are turning into heaps.

The first thing that is visible as one enters through the gate is a single-storey house with a neat tiled roof. On the right of the gate is a small pond surrounded by trees that create a screen of leaves. As one walks along the pathway, a larger house in the distance becomes visible through the leafy lattice work. It is a freshly painted double-storeyed house separated from the smaller one by a tiny field, where scores of little girls roam around. Beyond the field is a row of huge trees and glimmering through them is the Hooghly. The ghat is shaded by trees. Coconut trees rise way above the larger house.

This is the garden in Panihati where the child Rabindranath along with his family had sought refuge for some time during a dengue epidemic. That was the first time that the 12-year-old poet had ever left his Chitpur home to come face-to-face with nature and greenery in a Bengal village. Rabindranath's account of his stay is inscribed verbatim on a marble plaque installed next to the house with a tiled roof, under which stands a bust of the poet.

The mental picture conjured up by Rabindranath's lines comes very close to the reality. I visited the garden that once belonged to Chhatubabu or Asutosh Deb, the well-known merchant, on a monsoon evening, when the sun was setting in a blaze of red and gold. There is some controversy over the ownership of this beautiful property and Prashanta Pal had referred to it in his biography *Rabi Jibani*. He says Rabindranath had referred to this garden as being the property of one Lalababu, whose identity remains vague, although it is fairly clear that he is not the famous Krishnachandra Sinha of Paikpara Rajbari.

Rabindranath's niece Sarala Debi Chaudhurani had written that the property belonged to Debendranath Tagore, while rent bills available refer to the landlady Upendramohini Dassi. Her *annaprashan* or rice ceremony was held in the garden. Controversy apart, Chhatubabu himself had breathed his last here, his body touching the water of Hooghly to ensure his passage to heaven. It is said that Tagore had visited the garden much later in life as well.

Sunil Pal, 75, former chairman of Panihati municipality, says Lalchand Mallik had bought the garden from Chhatubabu, and later, Gopal Das Choudhury, the zamindar of Sherpur in Mymensinh, had acquired the property covering nine bighas. He opened a home for fallen women here which he named after his father, Gobinda Das. Now it is meant for underage girls from impoverished families.

Fig 8.1 *Trananath Banerjee's Kali temple*

The big house, where the 85 girls live, looks brand new. The original house was killed with care. A blue plaque declares that it is a "heritage building" but those who have repaired it have done more damage to it than vandals possibly could.

The roof was falling to pieces, so it was concretised. The capital of the Ionic columns has been transformed to something close to flattened lotus blossoms. The original wooden staircase was replaced by a concrete one some time ago. The fanlights were erased and much of the woodwork has been removed.

Behind the house is a magnificent Kali temple with five towers constructed by Trananath Banerjee, the local zamindar who had formed Panihati municipality way back in 1900. The street that passes by the home and the temple are named after this man who has no descendants. His house further down is occupied by squatters. Old men who sit on the ghat say that the temple had beautiful terracotta ornaments. Most of these were removed when the temple was repaired.

9

YOGAYOG (NEXUS) BY RABINDRANATH TAGORE

When the works of Rabindranath finally came out of copyright in the new millennium, there began a scramble among publishers to cash in on the brand name ' Tagore'. Rupa & Co immediately launched a series they called 'Rabindra Rachanavali' which merely recycled in attractive packaging the old and often substandard English translations of Tagore's books. These flawed — and sometimes abridged — translations were not revised, no notes were added, no editorial attempt was made to situate these texts of another era in their historical context and in most cases no mention was made of the fact that these are not new books, merely reprints of faded small-print editions earlier available under the Macmillan imprint. Unsuspecting readers who buy these elegant pocket-sized glossies are duped into thinking this is new-age Tagore in fresh English rendering to suit the temper of the present generation. But if they ever bother to read the volumes they purchase (the books make lovely gift items, and it is too tempting to pass them on) they would end up with the same impression that many Tagore readers in translation have had in the past: that he is an overrated writer, an icon for the Bengalis whose time is over. It is unfortunate that the opportunity for a fresh translation was passed over by Rupa in their haste to capture the market, although other publishers (e.g., Penguin, Srishti) have fared somewhat better.

Yogayog (Nexus) is in fact the only *new* translation of Tagore Rupa & Co have published, and it is so much superior to all the refurbished material they have been purveying so far, one wonders how this miracle happened. Given the total lack of editorial policy in their Rabindra Rachanavali series, it seems hardly likely that Rupa commissioned this translation in order to fill a gap in the corpus of Tagore translations in English. The chances are that it was a labour of love for the translator Hiten Bhaya, who incidentally has also translated Rabindranath's two books on Bangla language and on Linguistics entirely on his own initiative. Rupa probably accepted the manuscript offered to them without fully realising the value of what they had in their hands.

Of the eight novels written by Rabindranath (twelve, if one counts the novellas) *Yogayog* (first serialised in 1927-28) is the only one never translated into English before this. It is an unusually poignant but relatively less discussed text which has been overshadowed by the politically charged novels like *Gora* and *Ghare Bairey*. The politics in this novel is not of the nationalist variety — its historical context is the decline of the landed aristocracy in Bengal and the emergence of an enterpreneur class. Caught in the resultant clash of values, Kumudini is unable to see her path clearly. The last daughter of a family of refined taste but depleted resources, she is married to a self-made man proud of his enormous wealth. Nurtured by the mythology of Shiva-Sati, she was mentally prepared to love the abstract idea of a husband ignoring the crudeness of the actual man she was married to. But her admiration for her elder brother — also her mentor — creates a complication in the marital relationship. This elder brother Bipradas is an idealised character — liberal, intellectual, compassionate and artistic with an attractive aura of melancholy about him. His illness could be a metaphor for the precariousness of such a man's survival in the world of buying and selling. Unable to make money, he sinks deeper and deeper into debt until the entire family property gets irretrievably mortgaged to Kumudini's husband. Kumu is caught between her duty to her husband and her desire to be with her sick and distraught brother, nursing him, learning music from him and reading together. The husband and the brother are paradigmatically opposed characters — one obsessed with money and objects, the other like an incandescent flame, rising above the mundane. The grossness of the husband is further reinforced by his blatantly carnal relationship with his brother's widow while Kumudini is away from home. The novel ends with Kumu's discovery of her pregnancy — which compels her to go back to her husband. It is difficult to imagine a sadder resolution of her predicament. The biological entrapment of women ishighlighted with a ruthlessness unusual in writing from those pre-feminist days.

Yogayog is a powerful feminist text despite (or because of) the fact that it ends with a woman's defeat. Nora slamming the door and going out of the house was a potent image that heralded an entire movement, but the door closing in on Kumudini to imprison her for ever is a more searing statement. That it can be seen as a happy ending by most people around her makes it even more disturbing. Motir-ma, a staunch supporter of Kumu in her husband's house was nevertheless seriously upset at her declaration of independence: "Madhusudan may be absolutely unworthy of her, he may have been grievously wrong, but still he was a man. By virtue of being a man he was somewhere naturally superior to his wife — a fact that is unarguable. Can one win a case against our Maker? " Kumudini's pregnancy clinches Motir-ma's argument..

For a while Kumudini herself does not know what is the right course of action for her. She justifies her rebellion against her husband by identifying herself with Mirabai. She sings Mira's bhajans to calm herself but for her the 'giridhar nagar' does not become real. She tells her brother " ... if suffering is our inescapable lot, then we have to accept it and find a way of transcending it. That is why women stick to religion so desperately." The brother does not believe in religion; transcendence through music is enough for him. Music is repeatedly used as a sub-text in the novel — sometimes to create a mood, sometimes as a signifier for spirituality. One of the most memorable moments in the novel comes just before the end: brother and sister playing raag *bhairavi* on their esraj together, as the rays of the early morning sun pour on them through the flowering branches of gulmohur.

Bipradas, the brother is the only unqualified feminist in the novel who sees her sister's insult as the insult to all women, and insists that she stay on in the house on her own right, not a dependent on her brother. But this touching bond between the brother and sister foregrounded in the novel cannot distract us from the main issue — which is economic. Reading *Yogayog* in the new millennium it is difficult to ignore a historically situated romanticism that valorised spirit over body, other-worldliness over money and put on a pedestal the non-achiever who turns his back on worldly success. Instead of censuring Bipradas for not managing his property better, we are expected to admire his saintliness. One also notices a nostalgia for the vanishing landed gentry who were supposed to have been the custodians of art and refinement, and an unconcealed contempt for the crassness of new money. The present generation might question this crypto-feudal perspective, but it is necessary to recognize the inevitability that shaped this attitude at the beginning of the twentieth century, given the class composition of the literary community of the time.

Tagore's colour vision deficiency almost certainly inhibited and delayed his development as a visual artist. He never had the confidence to take formal lessons in art, though he encouraged his nephews, Abanindranath and Gaganendranth, to do so. He did not try to learn European-style naturalistic painting, though his own poetry of the 1890's and the writings of his nephew Balendranath Tagore from the same period, which were closely supervised and monitored by him, clearly show the influence of the female nude of classical Western art. Sushobhan's analysis of the influence of the female nude of Western art on Tagore's verse drama *Chitrangada* (1892) and on the poems of *Chitra* (1896), including 'Farewell to Heaven' and 'The Victorious Woman', poems I had myself translated, elicited my unreserved admiration. It was exciting to wander in the National Gallery of London with him, wondering which paintings Tagore might have seen with his own eyes during his visit there in 1890.

Most interestingly, though Tagore's poetry explored many stories and legends from Indian antiquity, he did not follow the parallel movement in art, the Bengal school, with its pale pastel colours and wash technique. Abanindranath excelled in this, but excellence in this technique could not be achieved by someone with a colour vision deficiency. Tagore felt a stronger attraction to Japanese art, which was linked to calligraphy, but the vigorous strokes of brush and ink needed for developing that style would have needed an enormous amount of training, for which Tagore had neither time nor patience. He found a route to art through primitivistic form-making, developed it through studying the woodcut, then developed it further by studying the way Expressionist artists were breaking all rules in the construction of forms and the application of colours. These studies gave him the confidence to become a painter in the fuller sense. He must have realized that his deficiency was no ultimate block; it could be bypassed. It was not necessary to be naturalistic in the use of either forms or colours. Amongst the plates in our book we have included some studies of faces with strikingly unconventional colouring. Real confidence in the use of colours came to him in the thirties, after he had successfully exhibited his pictures in Europe in 1930, and when he had had a substantial exposure to contemporary European art. Interestingly, as he gained confidence in the pictorial art, and in the use of colours in his pictures, he also gained a new vibrancy of colour language in his literary work. We have tried to make these connections. Sushobhan has traced some striking similarities in formal composition, and sometimes in colour composition, between some of Tagore's work and various examples of Expressionist art. These similarities, as well as the similarities between Tagore's work and exotic artefacts, are well illustrated in the plates in our book. Sometimes, as with certain paintings done by the Northern German Expressionist Emil Nolde and some done by Tagore, there is an intriguing similarity in composition, and even in the use of certain colours like yellow or violet, but Tagore's own use of reds is more muted. Tagore always referred to his art as a playful activity, playing with lines, splashing about with colours. Nevertheless, the range of colours in his paintings is limited. They exhibit a 'restricted colour space', in consonance with what one might expect of a protanopic artist.

10

RABINDRANATH'S TITANIC INTELLECT

Rabindranath's titanic intellect found manifestation in almost every facet of fine art. One of the most outstanding amongst them is Rabindra-sangeet, which embodies a breathtaking fusion of his musicianship and poetic genius. Such was the impact of this creation, that it not only withstood the test of time for more than a century, but also secured a unique place for itself in the subcontinent's musical culture.

The objective of this article is not to deliberate on the beauty and depth of Rabindra-sangeet. There are countless works in this regard by people far more knowledgeable on Rabindranath and Rabindra-sangeet, and the influence of Classical music on Rabindra Sangeet has been amply analyzed and now stands as an accepted fact. What this article aims to focus on, is how and to what extent has Rabindra-sangeet, in its turn, influenced the more traditional forms of music and its exponents. In particular, there has been a pronounced influence of Rabindra-sangeet on some of the noted classical instrumentalists of North India. There are indeed scopes of debate over the rationale and the extent of potential of this influence, but the fact remains that it cannot be denied. There are far too many precedents in its favor.

In the succeeding sections of this article, it has been attempted to investigate, what elements in Rabindra-sangeet triggered this kind of influence on Indian Classical instrumentalists and what consequences it led to.

It is an accepted fact that elements of Indian classical music have been used in an extremely intelligent and effective fashion in Rabindra-sangeet. It is indeed one of its most significant features. The application of this ingredient was however dictated principally by the perceived requirements of the mood evoked in the song, which was after all the core entity of his creation. An overt application of elements derived from classical music would have conflicted with this requirement. Therefore the application of classical elements, more often than not, had been subtle, and only to the extent necessary to express the emotive content of the song. Many of his songs therefore have only a partial conformity to ragas. Of course, in cases where he found the tonal color of the raga in almost total conformity to the sentiment of the song, he adopted the raga in its entirety. On certain instances, we even see authentic classical compositions adopted faithfully in respect of both melody and rhythm, set to outstanding Bengali lyric. The urge to evoke a particular mood to his own satisfaction, often led him to blend ragas in unexpectedly beautiful and interesting ways, or to look for uncharted and unexplored nuances within the known frameworks of ragas. It was on these occasions that some of his most beautiful and intellectually challenging creations came forth.

The influence of Rabindra-sangeet on Indian classical Instrumental music is perhaps due to the fact that much of what is played on Indian classical instruments today is derived from vocal music, principally of classical as also to some extent, of non classical origin (like lighter variety of compositions derived from folk music such as *Kirtan* or *Bhatiyali*). Classical instrumentalists have always looked for newer ideas and inspirations to feed their imagination not merely from these sources. Rabindra-sangeet with its sheer beauty and lyricism combined with the exquisite embodiment of the classical genre, naturally turns out to be a very potential resource to prospect.

The pioneering example in this regard was set by none other than the great Ustad Vilayat Khan Sahib. He had adopted the famous song, *Bhenge Mor Gharer Chabi,* into a beautiful, lilting light-classical composition. This was an interesting instance of a distinguished classical musician being motivated to imbibe the beauty and lyricism in Rabindra-sangeet .

The next example in this regard was set by Sri Buddhadev Dasgupta, the renowned sarodiya. Being a person with cultural roots in Bengal, he might have had a greater exposure to Rabindra-sangeet in general. His approach towards adoption of Rabindra-sangeet to classical music, naturally, was a more involved one. Out of the numerous classical compositions he has derived so far from Rabindra Sangeet, there are examples of transformations inspired by a variety of different aspects such as melodic appeal, interesting and unexpected application of raga movements, interesting ways of blending of ragas and even re-discovery of old classical compositions. His work in this area is based on years of exhaustive study and research in collaboration with Rabindra-sangeet experts like Shubhash Chowdhury.

The introduction of these kind of compositions in the arena of authentic Indian Classical Music took place over the decades of sixties and seventies. The initiation had been cautious and measured, considering the conventional mind-set of most of the contemporary musicians and listeners. For example, Sri Dasgupta played his first sarod composition, derived from the Rabindrasageet *Shedin dujone,* in his AIR National Program in 1978, dubbing it as a "light classical composition set to Pilu" and not as "a sarod gat based on Rabindra Sangeet".

It took quite some time for this novel approach to be accepted by the musicians, critics and listeners in its correct perspective. At the initial stage, presentation of such compositions were limited to more intimate gatherings rather than important and full fledged classical concerts. The response of the musical community, though not of outright rejection was somewhat confused. On one hand they were moved by the aesthetic appeal of the compositions, but on the other, were not quite sure of the categorization of such compositions. These compositions were definitely not like light classical compositions (commonly termed as "*dhun*"). Their appeal was definitely more dignified, and were set to purer forms of Ragas for the *Dhuns* are mostly set to lighter and blended Ragas with an ambience akin to that of folk music. They could also not be classified as authentic classical compositions or *bandishes* propagated over musical generations, as their origin was quite different. Sometimes they were sweepingly described as "Rabindra-sangeet played on sarod". This was a totally inappropriate description as well, as the compositions, more often than not, were quite different in their overall melodic construction, rythmic orientation and tempo than the original Rabindra-sangeet it had been derived from. In most cases the similarity was at a much more abstract level of melodic ideas and movements.

Therefore it was left to the proponents of this approach to educate and appraise the audience over the true characteristic of these compositions. This led to the formulation of certain experimental presentations featuring exponents of Rabindra-sangeet and classical musicians on a common stage, where some selected songs were presented along with their transformed versions of instrumental composition (or "*gat*" in the parlance of Hindusthani music), with adequate explanations in between. One of the earliest presentations of this kind was featured by Doordarshan Kendra, Calcutta with Budhhadev Dasgupta, V.Balsara (the famous pianist and film music personality) and Sri Ramanuj Dasgupta, (one of the contemporary upcoming Rabindra Sangeet singers). The reception to this program was very positive. Noted personalities from the sphere of Rabindra-sangeet as well as classical music acclaimed the effort. Further, as an interesting spin off, a large section of lay music-lovers and Tagore enthusiasts found an interesting cue towards the so-called "abstract" appeal of classical music. A number of similar experimental programs were staged over the following years, with other eminent personalities from spheres of classical music and Rabindra-sangeet, volunteering to take part in such ventures. There have been quite a few presentations of these nature featuring Suchitra Mitra and Budhhadev Dasgupta,

Subinoy Roy, Ravi Kichlu and Jaya Biswas and many others. Programs on this theme were accepted and presented by the AIR and Doordarshan on a number of occasions as well. Following suit, the Sangeet Natak Academy also funded a complete project on this theme. From this point onwards, it can be said, that the endeavor received its formal acceptance from the connoisseurs and listeners of classical music as also from the mass media. The idea was thereafter emulated by some of the most well known classical instrumentalists like Ustad Amjad Ali Khan. The trend continues to this day with dedicated stage programs focusing on classical compositions derived from Rabindra-sangeet. The interesting thing to note here is that just as the stage is shared by Rabindra-sangeet singers and classical instrumentalists, the galleries as well are shared by listeners of Rabindra-sangeet and classical music.

Having delineated the course of evolution of this interesting work, it would be worthwhile to take a closer look at the aspects of transformation that it involves. Since this has to be examined on the basis of concrete examples, the author has chosen a few, from the works of Sri Budhhadev Dasgupta, whose contribution in this regard has not only been a pioneering one, but perhaps also the most profound and exhaustive. The compositions derived by him had been based on a number of different perspectives of musical thinking.

It should be borne in mind that when we talk of transformation, we are obviously not talking about simply playing Rabindra-sangeet on sarod. Certain ideas are taken from the original Rabindra-sangeet and used to formulate a composition suitable for the context of a classical instrument. The original song therefore, undergoes a change or a sort of reconstruction in that certain salient ideas taken from the song are represented using the elements of sarod vocabulary. The resulting composition can consequently differ to a considerable extent from the orginal song that inspired its creation. The difference mostly is on counts of rhythmic construction or tempo but sometimes also in details of melodic construction. The similarity on the other hand is rather abstract and more often than not at the level of an overall melodic outline. There are a few examples of course, where the nature of the original song itself is so akin to that of a classical presentation that it finds its way almost unaltered into a classical composition.

As mentioned before, in many of his creations Rabindranath had focussed on ragas from rather striking and unexpected perspectives. Some of the movements he had used, though unusual, could not be challenged on counts of beauty and conformity to the raga. Some of these movements were taken from very old and traditional conventions in classical music. One such example is the use of R, G, M, P, D.., M G in the opening lines of *Shanti karo borishono*, based on Rag Tilak Kamod. From this took birth a beautiful, medium tempo (Madhya Laya) sarod composition (gat). An almost forgotten but exceedingly lyrical and romantic usage of Komal Gandhar in the latter part of the opening stanza (sthayee) of the song *Oi Janalar dhare* (Click here for an excerpt of the song or the *bandish* (Singer: Aniruddha Sinha; Ensemble: Sitar - Sugata Nag, Rahul Chatterjee, Sarod - Anirban Dasgupta, Pratyush Banerjee) is another outstanding example of such an application. In *Emono dine tare bola jai* we find a beautiful yet unconventional portrayal of Desh Malhar. Both of these songs have inspired excellent sarod gats set to teental. In some of the songs there has been an excellent delineation of uncommon Ragas. *Aji jato tara tabo akashe* (Excerpts: of the song or sarod-solo *bandish* . Artists: Sriradha Banerjee, sarod solo: Buddhadev Dasgupta) beautifully pictures Manjh Khambaj, a Raga which existed in the days of yore, but was somewhat rarely heard in the arena of pure classical music. This song was almost completely imbibed into an excellent slow teental (Vilambit) composition by Buddhadev, and has been rendered by him in many of his important concerts. (Excerpt: Anirban Dasgupta, Buddhadev Dasgupta and Zakir Hussain playing Manjh Khamaj at Vassar College, Poughkeepsie, 1985.) Incidentally, the same raga which Tagore so adeptly applied in his song, was later revived and popularised in the world of classical music by Acharya Alauddin Khan and his son, Ustad Ali Akbar Khan, the legendary sarodiya.

As mentioned before, many of the songs, have such a poignant and emotionally moving representation of commonly known ragas, that it would become rather difficult for a sensitive classical musician to overlook their intrinsic musicality. This poignancy or musicality in more objective terms can be interpreted as interesting application of note sequences. Many of the derived sarod compositions have been inspired by this factor. For example, in the song *Shedin dujone* one finds such an entrancing portrayal of the raga Pilu; here the notes of this rather common raga have been played with creative mastery. This was, in fact, Budhadev's first inspiration to derive a sarod composition from Rabindra sangeet. In "*Chokhe-r aaloey*" one finds a simple yet serenely beautiful depiction of Yaman Kalyan. This was converted into a medium tempo composition set to Teen tal. A scintillating fast Tintal composition of Khambaj was created from *Amar kantha hote gaan ke nilo*. The rhythm of the original song (Dadra) had to be entirely changed in order to adapt it to the ambience of an instrumental presentation. This was necessary as the idea was to present not just the song but a full-fledged classical composition derived out of it. The basis of this transformation was the beauty of the melodic outline of the song. In contrast, *Jodi e amaro* is a striking example where not only is the melodic construction but also the rhythmic framework has been followed in to-to in the derived instrumental composition based on raga Kafi. Here as well, Tagore entrances us with the rare, beautiful yet unmistakable approach to Kafi starting from the note *Dhaibat*. Out of Tagore's many songs based on Bhairabi, *Tabo daya* is one of the most outstanding considering the exquisite application of notes the heightens the expression of beauty and devotion. This prompted the creation of a medium tempo gat, largely maintaining the note sequences but changing the rhythmic framework to the somewhat-more-brisk Teen tal. There are more examples of this nature, such as *Shey kon boner horin* (Hemant) vocal [by Agnibha Banerjee] or instrumental *bandish* [by the "Ensemble"}, or *Shopney amar mone holo* (Hameer). vocal [by Aniruddha Sinha] or instrumental *bandish* [composed by the "Ensemble"].

Most of the songs composed by Rabindranath are characterised by their outstanding individuality, both from the point of views of lyric and melody. But on a certain instances we also find him faithfully adapting the melodic content of old classical compositions. In certain cases where he found the melodic as well as rhythmic orientation of existing or old classical compositions in keeping with the clime of the song being composed he never hesitated to follow them with complete faith. It was perhaps his tribute to a rich tradition of classical music. Hence in some of the songs like *Shukho hin nishi din*, (vocal [by Haimanti Shukla], sarod *bandish* [by Buddhadev Dasgupta] or *Shunyo hate phiri he* we find priceless classical *bandishes,* faithfully captured and set to outstanding poetry. Even playing these songs verbatim on an instrument would make them sound like authentic classical instrumental compositions. An interesting commentary on this is provided in the audio-cassette series named "Rupantori", featuring stalwarts like Subinoy Roy and Prasun Banerjee.

Sometimes, his flights of imagination had led Tagore to such emotional moods, that the tonal colors available from the basic ragas were not adequate to express them. Under such circumstances he used his artistic liberty to blend ragas. This resulted in masterful combination of some of the known ragas producing unforeseen melodic shades of the highest artistic order. One sees such a marriage between the ragas Todi and Bhairvi in the song *Rajani-r shesh tara*. Another unparalleled confluence of Bahar and Basant is noted in the song *Ami tomari shonge* (vocal [by Sriradha Banerjee] or *bandish* [by Buddhadev Dasgupta]). There may be many more examples. However, in the context of this discussion, it can be mentioned that both of these songs have provided potent ideas not only towards framing beautiful *bandishes* but also creating new kinds of blended ragas.

Evolution of new ideas in the realm of classical instrumental music inspired by Rabindra-sangeet is of more than incidental significance to some classical instrumentalists. An instrumentalist who has experienced, understood the classical appeal in Rabindra Sangeet and has succeeded in deriving useful ideas from it will obviously find his musical horizon widening much more than ever before. He will develop the insight to discover interesting and unknown corners of known ragas, which will not only apply to the derived compositions but also to the more conventional aspects of his playing like Alap and Vistar. At a more abstract level it might also have significant effects and possibly improvements on his perspective of thinking on ragas. The derived compositions, which as metioned before, have a very distinctive aesthetic ambience would considerably expand his repertoire. He will find himself in possession the magic key to an inexhaustible repository of ideas.

It is a known fact that classical musicians over all ages and centuries have derived musical ideas from classical as well as non-classical sources. In a sense, therefore, this example of Rabindra-sangeet inspiring creation of classical compositions may be interpreted as a repetition of history. However, a closer look suggests a difference. This lies in the artistic maturity of the source material in this case, so that a strong temptation to plagiarize must be resisted and the essence gleaned, and this can be an extremely challenging task.

Also, this endeavour has encouraged an interesting cross-influence. Some of the classical musicians have come down from their ivory towers and given Rabindra-sangeet its much overdue recognition. The exponents of Rabindra-sangeet by and large have welcomed this dialogue between these two islands of India's musical culture which were so far largely isolated from each other. For classical instrumentalists it opened up an extremely potent resource to excavate for newer ideas which are applicable to their own realm. Finally, the subtle yet long-term consequence could be to motivate future generations of musicians to enrich the realm of Classical Music from similar sources beyond the boundary their own domain.

11

AWARD CEREMONY SPEECH

In awarding the Nobel Prize in Literature to the Anglo-Indian poet, Rabindranath Tagore, the Academy has found itself in the happy position of being able to accord this recognition to an author who, in conformity with the express wording of Alfred Nobel's last will and testament, had during the current year, written the finest poems «of an idealistic tendency.» Moreover, after exhaustive and conscientious deliberation, having concluded that these poems of his most nearly approach the prescribed standard, the Academy thought that there was no reason to hesitate because the poet's name was still comparatively unknown in Europe, due to the distant location of his home. There was even less reason since the founder of the Prize laid it down in set terms as his «express wish and desire that, in the awarding of the Prize, no consideration should be paid to the nationality to which any proposed candidate might belong.

Tagore's *Gitanjali: Song Offerings* (1912), a collection of religious poems, was the one of his works that especially arrested the attention of the selecting critics. Since last year the book, in a real and full sense, has belonged to English literature, for the author himself, who by education and practice is a poet in his native Indian tongue, has bestowed upon the poems a new dress, alike perfect in form and personally original in inspiration. This has made them accessible to all in England, America, and the entire Western world for whom noble literature is of interest and moment. Quite independently of any knowledge of his Bengali poetry, irrespective, too, of differences of religious faiths, literary schools, or party aims, Tagore has been hailed from various quarters as a new and admirable master of that poetic art which has been a never-failing concomitant of the expansion of British civilization ever since the days of Queen Elizabeth. The features of this poetry that won immediate and enthusiastic admiration are the perfection with which the poet's own ideas and those he has borrowed have been harmonized into a complete whole; his rhythmically balanced style, that, to quote an English critic's opinion, «combines at once the feminine grace of poetry with the virile power of prose»; his austere, by some termed classic, taste in the choice of words and his use of the other elements of expression in a borrowed tongue - those features, in short, that stamp an original work as such, but which at the same time render more difficult its reproduction in another language.

The same estimate is true of the second cycle of poems that came before us, *The Gardener, Lyrics of Love and Life* (1913). In this work, however, as the author himself points out, he has recast rather than interpreted his earlier inspirations. Here we see another phase of his personality, now subject to the alternately blissful and torturing experiences of youthful love, now prey to the feelings of longing and joy that the vicissitudes of life give rise to, the whole interspersed nevertheless with glimpses of a higher world.

English translations of Tagore's prose stories have been published under the title *Glimpses of Bengal Life* (1913). Though the form of these tales does not bear his own stamp - the rendering being by another hand - their content gives evidence of his versatility and wide range of observation, of his heartfelt sympathy with the fates and experiences of differing types of men, and of his talent for plot construction and development.

Tagore has since published both a collection of poems, poetic pictures of childhood and home life, symbolically entitled

The Crescent Moon (1913), and a number of lectures given before American and English university audiences, which in book form he calls *Sâdhanâ: The Realisation of Life* (1913). They embody his views of the ways in which man can arrive at a faith in the light of which it may be possible to live. This very seeking of his to discover the true relation between faith and thought makes Tagore stand out as a poet of rich endowment, characterized by his great profundity of thought, but most of all by his warmth of feeling and by the moving power of his figurative language. Seldom indeed in the realm of imaginative literature are attained so great a range and diversity of note and of colour, capable of expressing with equal harmony and grace the emotions of every mood from the longing of the soul after eternity to the joyous merriment prompted by the innocent child at play.

Concerning our understanding of this poetry, by no means exotic but truly universally human in character, the future will probably add to what we know now. We do know, however, that the poet's motivation extends to the effort of reconciling two spheres of civilization widely separated, which above all is the characteristic mark of our present epoch and constitutes its most important task and problem. The true inwardness of this work is most clearly and purely revealed in the efforts exerted in the Christian mission-field throughout the world. In times to come, historical inquirers will know better how to appraise its importance and influence, even in what is at present hidden from our gaze and where no or only grudging recognition is accorded. They will undoubtedly form a higher estimate of it than the one now deemed fitting in many quarters. Thanks to this movement, fresh, bubbling springs of living water have been tapped, from which poetry in particular may draw inspiration, even though those springs are perhaps intermingled with alien streams, and whether or not they be traced to their right source or their origin be attributed to the depths of the dreamworld. More especially, the preaching of the Christian religion has provided in many places the first definite impulse toward a revival and regeneration of the vernacular language, i.e., its liberation from the bondage of an artificial tradition, and consequently also toward a development of its capacity for nurturing and sustaining a vein of living and natural poetry.

The Christian mission has exercised its influence as a rejuvenating force in India, too, where in conjunction with religious revivals many of the vernaculars were early put to literary use, thereby acquiring status and stability. However, with only too regular frequency, they fossilized again under pressure from the new tradition that gradually established itself. But the influence of the Christian mission has extended far beyond the range of the actually registered proselytizing work. The struggle that the last century witnessed between the living vernaculars and the sacred language of ancient times for control over the new literatures springing into life would have had a very different course and outcome, had not the former found able support in the fostering care bestowed upon them by the self-sacrificing missionaries.

It was in Bengal, the oldest Anglo-Indian province and the scene many years before of the indefatigable labours of that missionary pioneer, Carey, to promote the Christian religion and to improve the vernacular language, that Rabindranath Tagore was born in 1861. He was a scion of a respected family that had already given evidence of intellectual ability in many areas. The surroundings in which the boy and young man grew up were in no sense primitive or calculated to hem in his conceptions of the world and of life. On the contrary, in his home there prevailed, along with a highly cultivated appreciation of art, a profound reverence for the inquiring spirit and wisdom of the forefathers of the race, whose texts were used for family devotional worship. Around him, too, there was then coming into being a new literary spirit that consciously sought to reach forth to the people and to make itself acquainted with their life needs. This new spirit gained in force as reforms ere firmly effected by the Government, after the quelling of the widespread, confused Indian Mutiny.

Rabindranath's father was one of the leading and most zealous members of a religious community to which his son still belongs. That body, known by the name of «Brahmo Samaj», did not arise as a sect of the ancient Hindu type, with the purpose of spreading the worship of some particular godhead as superior to all others. Rather, it was founded in the early part of the nineteenth century by an enlightened and influential man who had been much impressed by the doctrines of Christianity, which he had studied also in England. He endeavoured to give to the native Hindu traditions, handed down from the past, an interpretation in agreement with what he conceived to be the spirit and import of the Christian faith. Doctrinal controversy has since been rife regarding the interpretation of truth that he and his successors were thus led to give, whereby the community has been subdivided into a number of independent sects. The character, too, of the community, appealing essentially to highly trained intellectual minds, has from its inception always precluded any large growth of the numbers of its avowed adherents. Nevertheless, the indirect influence exercised by the body, even upon the development of popular education and literature, is held to be very considerable indeed. Among those community members who have grown up in recent years, Rabindranath Tagore has laboured to a pre-eminent degree. To them he has stood as a revered master and prophet. That intimate interplay of teacher and pupil so earnestly sought after has attained a deep, hearty, and simple manifestation, both in religious life and in literary training.

To carry out his life's work Tagore equipped himself with a many-sided culture, European as well as Indian, extended and matured by travels abroad and by advanced study in London. In his youth he travelled widely in his own land, accompanying his father as far as the Himalayas. He was still quite young when he began to write in Bengali, and he has tried his hand in prose and poetry, lyrics and dramas. In addition to his descriptions of the life of he common people of his own country, he has dealt in separate works with questions in literary criticism, philosophy, and sociology. At one period, some time ago, there occurred a break in the busy round of his activities, for he then felt obliged, in accord with immemorial practice among his race, to pursue for a time a contemplative hermit life in a boat floating on the waters of a tributary of the sacred Ganges River. After he returned to ordinary life, his reputation among his own people as a man of refined wisdom and chastened piety grew greater from day to day. The open-air school which he established in western Bengal, beneath the sheltering branches of the mango tree, has brought up numbers of youths who as devoted disciples have spread his teaching throughout the land. To this place he has now retired, after spending nearly a year as an honoured guest in the literary circles of England and America and attending the Religious History Congress held in Paris last summer (1913).

Wherever Tagore has encountered minds open to receive his high teaching, the reception accorded him has been that suited to a bearer of good tidings which are delivered, in language intelligible to all, from that treasure house of the East whose existence had long been conjectured. His own attitude, moreover, is that he is but the intermediary, giving freely of that to which by birth he has access. He is not at all anxious to shine before men as a genius or as an inventor of some new thing. In contrast to the cult of work, which is the product of life in the fenced-in cities of the Western world, with its fostering of a restless, contentious spirit; in contrast to its struggle to conquer nature for the love of gain and profit, «as if we are living», Tagore says, «in a hostile world where we have to wrest everything we want from an unwilling and alien arrangement of things» (*Sâdhanâ*, p. 5); in contrast to all that enervating hurry and scurry, he places before us the culture that in the vast, peaceful, and enshrining forests of India attains its perfection, a culture that seeks primarily the quiet peace of the soul in ever-increasing harmony with the life of nature herself It is a poetical, not a historical, picture that Tagore here reveals to us to confirm his promise that a peace awaits us, too. By virtue of the right associated with the gift of prophecy, he freely depicts the scenes that have loomed before his creative vision at a period contemporary with the beginning of time.

He is, however, as far removed as anyone in our midst from all that we are accustomed to hear dispensed and purveyed in the market places as Oriental philosophy, from painful dreams about the transmigration of souls and the impersonal *karma*, from the pantheistic, and in reality abstract, belief that is usually regarded as peculiarly characteristic of the higher civilization in India. Tagore himself is not even prepared to admit that a belief of that description can claim any authority from the profoundest utterances of the wise men of the past. He peruses his Vedic hymns, his *Upanishads*, and indeed the theses of Buddha himself, in such a manner that he discovers in them, what is for him an irrefutable truth. If he seeks the divinity in nature, he finds there a living personality with the features of omnipotence, the all-embracing lord of nature, whose preternatural spiritual power nevertheless likewise reveals its presence in all temporal life, small as well as great, but especially in the soul of man predestined for eternity. Praise, prayer, and fervent devotion pervade the song offerings that he lays at the feet of this nameless divinity of his. Ascetic and even ethic austerity would appear to be alien to his type of divinity worship, which may be characterized as a species of aesthetic theism. Piety of that description is in full concord with the whole of his poetry, and it has bestowed peace upon him. He proclaims the coming of that peace for weary and careworn souls even within the bounds of Christendom.

This is mysticism, if we like to call it so, but not a mysticism that, relinquishing personality, seeks to become absorbed in an All that approaches a Nothingness, but one that, with all the talents and faculties of the soul trained to their highest pitch, eagerly sets forth to meet the living Father of the whole creation. This more strenuous type of mysticism was not wholly unknown even in India before the days of Tagore, hardly indeed among the ascetics and philosophers of ancient times but rather in the many forms of *bhakti*, a piety whose very essence is the profound love of and reliance upon God. Ever since the Middle Ages, influenced in some measure by the Christian and other foreign religions, *bhakti* has sought the ideals of its faith in the different phases of Hinduism, varied in character but each to all intents monotheistic in conception. All those higher forms of faith have disappeared or have been depraved past recognition, choked by the superabundant growth of that mixture of cults that has attracted to its banner all those Indian peoples who lacked an adequate power of resistance to its blandishments. Even though Tagore may have borrowed one or another note from the orchestral symphonies of his native predecessors, yet he treads upon firmer ground in this age that draws the peoples of the earth closer together along paths of peace, and of strife too, to joint and collective responsibilities, and that spends its own energies in dispatching greetings and good wishes far over land and sea. Tagore, though, in thought-impelling pictures, has shown us how all things temporal are swallowed up in the eternal:

Time is endless in thy hands, my lord.

There is none to count thy minutes.

Days and nights pass and ages bloom and fade like lowers. Thou knowest how to wait.

Thy centuries follow each other perfecting a small wild flower.

We have no time to lose, and having no time, we must scramble for our chances. We are too poor to be late. And thus it is that time goes try, while I give it to every querulous man who claims it, and thine altar is empty of all offerings to the last.

At the end of the day I hasten in fear lest thy gate be shut; but if I find that yet there is time.

12

GREATEST WRITER IN MODERN INDIAN LITERATURE

Greatest writer in modern Indian literature, Bengali poet, novelist, educator, and an early advocate of Independence for India. Tagaore won the Nobel Prize for Literature in 1913. Two years later he was awarded the knighthood, but he surrendered it in 1919 as a protest against the Massacre of Amritsar, where British troops killed some 400 Indian demonstrators. Tagore's influence over Gandhi and the founders of modern India was enormous, but his reputation in the West as a mystic has perhaps mislead his Western readers to ignore his role as a reformer and critic of colonialism.

"When one knows thee, then alien there is none, then no door is shut. Oh, grant me my prayer that I may never lose touch of the one in the play of the many." **(from *Gitanjali*)**

Rabindranath Tagore was born in Calcutta into a wealthy and prominent family. His father was Maharishi Debendranath Tagore, a religious reformer and scholar. His mother, Sarada Devi, died when Tagore was very young - he realized that she will never come back was when her body was carried through a gate to a place where it was burned. Tagore's grandfather had established a huge financial empire for himself. He helped a number of public projects, such as Calcutta Medical College.

The Tagores tried to combine traditional Indian culture with Western ideas; all the children contributed significantly to Bengali literature and culture. However, in *My Reminiscences* Tagore mentions that it was not until the age of ten when he started to use socks and shoes. And servants beat the children regularly. Tagore, the youngest, started to compose poems at the age of eight. Tagore's first book, a collection of poems, appeared when he was 17; it was published by Tagore's friend who wanted to surprise him.

Tagore received his early education first from tutors and then at a variety of schools. Among them were Bengal Academy where he studied history and culture. At University College, London, he studied law but left after a year - he did not like the weather. Once he gave a beggar a cold coin - it was more than the beggar had expected and he returned it. In England Tagore started to compose the poem 'Bhagna Hridaj' (a broken heart).

In 1883 Tagore married Mrinalini Devi Raichaudhuri, with whom he had two sons and three daughters. In 1890 Tagore moved to East Bengal (now Bangladesh), where he collected local legends and folklore. Between 1893 and 1900 he wrote seven volumes of poetry, including SONAR TARI (The Golden Boat), 1894 and KHANIKA, 1900. This was highly productive period in Tagore's life, and earned him the rather misleading epitaph 'The Bengali Shelley.' More important was that Tagore wrote in the common language of the people. This also was something that was hard to accept among his critics and scholars.

Tagore was the first Indian to bring an element of psychological realism to his novels. Among his early major prose works are CHOCHER BALI (1903, Eyesore) and NASHTANIR (1901, The Broken Nest), published first serially. Between 1891 and 1895 he published forty-four short stories in Bengali periodical, most of them in the monthly journal *Sadhana* .

Especially Tagore's short stories influenced deeply Indian Literature. 'Punishment', a much anthologized work, was set in a rural village. It describes the oppression of women through the tragedy of the low-caste Rui family. Chandara is a proud, beautiful woman, "buxom, well-rounded, compact and sturdy," her husband, Chidam, is a farm-laborer, who works in the fields with his brother Dukhiram. One day when they return home after whole day of toil and humiliation, Dukhiram kills in anger his sloppy and slovenly wife because his food was not ready. To help his brother, Chidam's tells to police that his wife struck her sister-in-law with the farm-knife. Chandara takes the blame on to herself. 'In her thoughts, Chandara was saying to her husband, "I shall give my youth to the gallows instead of you. My final ties in this life will be with them."' Afterwards both Chidam and Dukhiram try to confess that they were quilty but Chandara is convicted. Just before the hanging, the doctor says that her husband wants to see her. "To hell with him," says Chandara.

In 1901 Tagore founded a school outside Calcutta, Visva-Bharati, which was dedicated to emerging Western and Indian philosophy and education. It become a university in 1921. He produced poems, novels, stories, a history of India, textbooks, and treatises on pedagogy. Tagore's wife died in 1902, next year one of his daughters died, and in 1907 Tagore lost his younger son.

Tagore's reputation as a writer was established in the United States and in England after the publication of GITANJALI: SONG OFFERINGS, about divine and human love. The poems were translated into English by the author himself. In the introduction from 1912 William Butler Yates wrote: "These lyrics - which are in the original, my Indians tell me, full of subtlety of rhythm, of untranslatable delicacies of colour, of metrical invention - display in their thought a world I have dreamed of all my life long." Tagore's poems were also praised by Ezra Pound , and drew the attention of the Nobel Prize committee. "There is in him the stillness of nature. The poems do not seem to have been produced by storm or by ignition, but seem to show the normal habit of his mind. He is at one with nature, and finds no contradictions. And this is in sharp contrast with the Western mode, where man must be shown attempting to master nature if we are to have "great drama." (Ezra Pound in *Fortnightly Review* , 1 March 1913) However, Tagore also experimented with poetic forms and these works have lost much in translations into other languages.

Much of Tagore's ideology come from the teaching of the Upahishads and from his own beliefs that God can be found through personal purity and service to others. He stressed the need for new world order based on transnational values and ideas, the "unity consciousness." "The soil, in return for her service, keeps the tree tied to her; the sky asks nothing and leaves it free." Politically active in India, Tagore was a supporter of Gandhi, but warned of the dangers of nationalistic thought. Unable to gain ideological support to his views, he retired into relative solitude. Between the years 1916 and 1934 he travelled widely. From his journey to Japan in 1916 he produced articles and books. In 1927 he toured in Southeast Asia. *Letters from Java* , which first was serialized in *Vichitra* , was issued as a book, JATRI, in 1929. His Majesty, Riza Shah Pahlavi, invited Tagore to Iran in 1932. On his journeys and lecture tours Tagore attempted to spread the ideal of uniting East and West. While in Japan he wrote: "The Japanese do not waste their energy in useless screaming and quarreling, and because there is no waste of energy it is not found wanting when required. This calmness and fortitude of body and mind is part of their national self-realization."

Tagore wrote his most important works in Bengali, but he often translated his poems into English. At the age of 70 Tagore took up painting. He was also a composer, settings hundreds of poems to music. Many of his poems are actually songs, and inseparable from their music. Tagore's 'Our Golden Bengal' became the national anthem of Bangladesh. Only hours before he died on August 7, in 1941, Tagore dictated his last poem. His written production, still not completely collected, fills nearly 30 substantial volumes. Tagore remained a well-known and popular author in the West until the end of the 1920s, but nowadays he is not so much read.

India's National Movement for freedom was accompanied by a large wave of social, educational and economic awareness throughout the nation. Tagore, one of the foremost thinkers in the country at the time spent time in building educational infrastructure. A man of true talent, his contribution to the freedom movement is significant. Gandhi has called him Gurudev (The Supreme Teacher). ve us our national anthem wrote - " I have loved India and sought to serve her not because of her geographical magnitude, not because of her great past, but because of my faith in her today and my belief that she will stand for truth and freedom and the higher things of life".

The Song of Free India

Where the mind is without fear and the head is held high;

Where knowledge is free;

Where the world has not been broken up into fragments by narrow domestic walls;

Where the words come out from the depth of truth;

Where tireless striving stretches its arms towards perfection;

Where the clear stream of reason has not lost its way into the dreary desert sand of dead habit;

Where the mind is led forward by Thee into ever-widening thought and action— Into that heaven of freedom, my Father, let my country awake.

The National Anthem

The song Jana-gana-mana, composed originally in Bengali by Rabindranath Tagore, was adopted in its Hindi version by the Constituent Assembly as the national anthem of India on 24 January 1950. It was first sung on 27 December 1911 at the Calcutta Session of the Indian National Congress. The complete song consists of five stanzas. The first stanza contains the full version of the National Anthem :

Jana-gana-mana-adhinayaka, jaya he

Bharata-bhagya-vidhata.
Punjab-Sindh-Gujarat-Maratha
Dravida-Utkala-Banga
Vindhya-Himachala-Yamuna-Ganga
Uchchala-Jaladhi-taranga.
Tava shubha name jage,
Tava shubha asisa mage,
Gahe tava jaya gatha,
Jana-gana-mangala-dayaka jaya he
Bharata-bhagya-vidhata.
Jaya he, jaya he, jaya he,
Jaya jaya jaya, jaya he!

Selected works:

KABIKAHINI, 1878 - A Poet's Tale
SADHYA SANGEET, 1882 - Evening Songs
PRABHAT SANGEET, 1883 - Morning Songs
BAU-THAKURANIR HAT, 1883
RAJASHI, 1887
RAJA O RANI, 1889 - The King and the Queen / Devouring Love
VISARGAN, 1890 - Sacrifice
MANASI, 1890
IUROPE-JATRIR DIARI, 1891, 1893
VALMIKI PRATIBHA, 1893
SONAR TARI, 1894 - The Golden Boat
KHANIKA, 1900 - Moments
KATHA, 1900
KALPANA, 1900
NAIVEDYA, 1901
NASHTANIR, 1901 - The Broken Nest
SHARAN, 1902
BINODINI, 1902
CHOCHER BALI, 1903 - Eyesore
NAUKADUBI, 1905 - Haaksirikko

KHEYA, 1906

NAUKADUBI, 1906 - The Wreck

GORA, 1907-09 - suom.

SARADOTSAVA, 1908 - Autumn Festival

GALPAGUCCHA, 1912 - A Bunch of Stories

CHINNAPATRA, 1912

VIDAY-ABHISAP, 1912 - The Curse at Farewell

GITANJALI, 1912 - Song Offerings (new translation in 2000 by Joen Winter, publ. Anvil Press) - Uhrilauluja

JIBAN SMRTI, 1912 - My Reminiscenes - Elämäni muistoja , trans. by J. Hollo

DAKGHAR, 1912 - Post Office

The Crescent Moon, 1913

Glimpses of Bengal Life, 1913

The Hungry Stones and Other Stories, 1913

CHITRA, 1914 - transl.

GHITIMALAYA, 1914

The King of the Dark Chamber, 1914

The Post Office, 1914

Sadhana, 1914

GHARE-BAIRE, 1916 - The Home and the World - Koti ja maailma

BALAK, 1916 - A Flight of Swans

CHATURANGA, 1916 - transl.

Fruit Gathering, 1916

The Hungry Stones, 1916

Stray Birds, 1916

PERSONALITY, 1917 - Persoonallisuus

The Cycle of Spring, 1917

Sacrifice, and Other Plays, 1917

My Reminiscene, 1917

Nationalism, 1917

Mashi and Other Stories, 1918

Stories from Tagore, 1918
PALATAKA, 1918
JAPAN-JATRI, 1919 - A Visit to Japan
Greater India, 1921
The Fugitive, 1921
Creative Unity, 1921
LIPIKA, 1922
MUKTADHARA, 1922 - trans.
Poems, 1923
Gora, 1924
Letters from Abroad, 1924
Red Oleander, 1924
GRIHAPRABESH, 1925
Broken Ties and Other Stories, 1925
Rabindranath Tagore: Twenty-Two Poems, 1925
RAKTA-KARABI, 1925 - Red Oleanders
SADHANA, 1926 - suom.
NATIR PUJA, 1926 - transl.
Letters to a Friend, 1928
SESHER KAVITA, 1929 - Farewell, My Friend
MAHUA, 1929 - The Herald of Spring
JATRI, 1929
YAGAYOG, 1929
The Religion of Man, 1930
The Child, 1931
RASHIAR CHITHI, 1931 - Letters from Russia
PATRAPUT, 1932
PUNASCHA, 1932
Mahatmahi and the Depressed Humanity, 1932
The Golden Boat, 1932
Sheaves, Poems and Songs, 1932
DUI BON, 1933 - Two Sisters

CHANDALIKA, 1933 - transl.
MALANCHA, 1934 - The Garden
CHAR ADHYAYA, 1934 - Four Chapters
BITHIKA, 1935
SHESH SAPTAK, 1935
PATRAPUT, 1936
SYAMALI, 1936 - trans.
Collected Poems and Plays, 1936
KHAPCHARA, 1937
SEMJUTI, 1938
PRANTIK, 1938
PRAHASINI, 1939
PATHER SANCAY, 1939
AKASPRADIP, 1939
SYAMA, 1939
NABAJATAK, 1940
SHANAI, 1940
CHELEBELA, 1940 - My Boyhood Days
ROGSHAJYAY, 1940
AROGYA, 1941
JANMADINE, 1941
GALPASALPA, 1941
Last Poems, 1941
The Parrots Training, 1944
Rolland and Tagore, 1945
Three Plays, 1950
Crisis in Civilization, 1950
Sheaves, 1951
More Stories from Tagore, 1951
A Tagore's Testament, 1955
Our Universe, 1958
The Runaway and Other Stories, 1959
Wings of Death, 1960

GITABITAN, 1960
A Tagore Reader, 1961 (ed. by Amiya Chakravarty)
Towards Universal Man, 1961
On Art and Aesthetics, 1961
BICITRA, 1961
GALPAGUCCHA, 1960-62 (4 vols.)
Boundless Sky, 1964
The Housewarming, 1964
RABINDRA-RACANABALI, 1964-1966 (27 vols.)
Patraput, 1969
Imperfect Encounter, 1972
Later Poems, 1974
The Housewarming, 1977
Rabindranath Tagore: Selected Poems, 1985
Rabindranath Tagore: Selected Short Stories, 1991 (trans. by William Radice)